1920–1940

The Twentieth Century

Other books in the
Events That Changed the World series:

1900–1920
1940–1960
1960–1980
1980–2000

1920–1940

The Twentieth Century

Sharon M. Himsl, *Book Editor*

Daniel Leone, *President*
Bonnie Szumski, *Publisher*
Scott Barbour, *Managing Editor*

San Diego • Detroit • New York • San Francisco • Cleveland
New Haven, Conn. • Waterville, Maine • London • Munich

For more information, contact
Greenhaven Press
27500 Drake Rd.
Farmington Hills, MI 48331-3535
Or you can visit our Internet site at http://www.gale.com

Cover credit: © CORBIS
Franklin Delano Roosevelt Library, 133
Library of Congress, 16, 36, 61, 104, 162
National Archives, 19, 22
USHMM Photo Archives, 111

LIBRARY OF CONGRESS CATALOGING-IN-PUBLICATION DATA

1920–1940 / Sharon M. Himsl, book editor.
p. cm. — (Events that changed the world)
Includes bibliographical references and index.
ISBN 0-7377-1755-6 (pbk. : alk. paper) —
ISBN 0-7377-1754-8 (lib. bdg. : alk. paper)
1. World politics—1919–1932. 2. World politics—1933–1945. 3. Fascism—History—20th century. 4. Nationalism—History—20th century. 5. Popular culture—History—20th century. I. Himsl, Sharon M. II. Series.
D720.A13 2004
909.82'2—dc21 2003044864

Printed in the United States of America

CONTENTS

FOREWORD

In 1543 a Polish astronomer named Nicolaus Copernicus published a book entitled *De revolutionibus orbium coelestium* in which he theorized that Earth revolved around the Sun. In 1688, during the Glorious Revolution, Dutch prince William of Orange invaded England and overthrew King James II. In 1922 Irish author James Joyce's novel *Ulysses*, which describes one day in Dublin, was published.

Although these events are seemingly unrelated, occurring in different nations and in different centuries, they all share the distinction of having changed the world. Although Copernicus's book had a relatively minor impact at the time of its publication, it eventually had a momentous influence. The Copernican system provided a foundation on which future scientists could develop an accurate understanding of the solar system. Perhaps more importantly, it required humanity to contemplate the possibility that Earth, far from occupying a special place at the center of creation, was merely one planet in a vast universe. In doing so, it forced a reevaluation of the Christian cosmology that had served as the foundation of Western culture. As professor Thomas S. Kuhn writes, "The drama of Christian life and the morality that had been made dependent upon it would not readily adapt to a universe in which the earth was just one of a number of planets."

Like the Copernican revolution, the Glorious Revolution of 1688–1689 had a profound influence on the future of Western societies. By deposing James II, William and his wife, Mary, ended the Stuart dynasty, a series of monarchs who had favored the Catholic Church and had limited the power of Parliament for decades. Under William and Mary, Parliament passed the Bill of Rights, which established the legislative supremacy of Parliament and barred Roman Catholics from the throne. These actions initiated the gradual process by which the power of the government of England shifted from the monarchy to Parliament, establishing a democratic system that would be copied, with some variations, by the United States and other democratic societies worldwide.

Whereas the Glorious Revolution had a major impact in the political sphere, the publication of Joyce's novel *Ulysses* represented a revolution in literature. In an effort to capture the sense of chaos and discontinuity that permeated the culture in the wake of World War I, Joyce did away with the use of straightforward narrative that had dominated fiction up to that time. The novel, whose structure mirrors that of Homer's *Odyssey*, combines realistic descriptions of events with passages that convey the characters' inner experience by means of a technique known as stream of consciousness, in which the characters' thoughts and feelings are presented without regard to logic or narrative order. Due to its departure from the traditional modes of fiction, *Ulysses* is often described as one of the seminal works of modernist literature. As stated by Pennsylvania State University professor Michael H. Begnal, "*Ulysses* is the novel that changed the direction of 20th-century fiction written in English."

Copernicus's theory of a sun-centered solar system, the Glorious Revolution, and James Joyce's *Ulysses* are just three examples of time-bound events that have had far-reaching effects—for better or worse—on the progress of human societies worldwide. History is made up of an inexhaustible list of such events. In the twentieth century alone, for example, one can isolate any number of world-shattering moments: the first performance of Igor Stravinsky's ballet *The Rites of Spring* in 1913; Japan's attack on Pearl Harbor on December 7, 1941; the launch of the satellite *Sputnik* on October 4, 1957. These events variously influenced the culture, society, and political configuration of the twentieth century.

Greenhaven Press's Events That Changed the World series is designed to help readers learn about world history by examining seemingly random events that have had the greatest influence on the development of cultures, societies, and governments throughout the ages. The series is divided into sets of several anthologies, with each set covering a period of one hundred years. Each volume begins with an introduction that provides essential context on the time period being covered. Then, the major events of the era are covered by means of primary and secondary sources. Primary sources include firsthand accounts, speeches, correspondence, and other materials that bring history alive. Secondary sources analyze the profound effects the events had on the world. Each reading is preceded by an introduction that puts it in context and emphasizes the event's importance in the ongoing evolution of world history. Additional features add to the value of the series: An annotated table of contents and an index allow readers to quickly locate material of interest. A chronology provides an easy reference for contextual information. And a bibliography offers opportunities for further exploration. All of these features help to make the Events That Changed the World series a valuable resource for readers interested in the major events that have shaped the course of humanity.

INTRODUCTION

Of all of the events that occurred during the scant twenty years between 1920 and 1940, by far some of the most transforming had to do with advances in technology, transportation, and communications. Some of these inventions would have tremendous social and economic implications that would change the way much of the world lived, worked, and played. All would serve to draw the world closer, and many in the world would come to depend upon these advances like never before.

Electricity

The fuel behind this rapid modernization was the use of electricity. Usage in the United States nearly doubled in the twenties and tripled by the end of the thirties. Electrical appliances such as toasters, egg beaters, grills, waffle irons, percolators, refrigerators, and washing machines were developed to support this new fuel transforming the way people did their chores at home.

Industry was equally impacted by electrification. Most industries converted to electrical power by the end of the twenties, enabling factories to use the latest technology in machinery and automation. For example, the electrical assembly line pioneered by automobile builder Henry Ford was widely adopted by industries in the 1920s and 1930s. The assembly line and electrical machinery created new jobs and opportunities for those able to learn new skills.

Those who benefited most from electricity lived in the cities, where urban use rose sharply from 47 percent in 1920 to 85 percent in 1930. Rural use only rose from 1.6 percent to 10 percent in comparison, but a government program called the Rural Electrification Administration sped electricity to remote areas. As David E. Kyvig writes in his book *Daily Life in the United States, 1920–1939*, "These indeed were the decades during which American domestic life became electrified."[1]

Automobiles

Another invention that brought about widespread change was the automobile. "By 1923 the automobile had become a necessity, and everybody, regardless of social or financial position, had to have one,"[2] contends Frederick Lewis Allen in his book *Only Yesterday*. Part of the automobile's popularity during the twenties was due to Henry Ford's mass production of the Model T Ford, popularly named the Tin Lizzie, which made cars available at the low price of three hundred dollars.

The motor vehicle industry had a tremendous impact on the economy in the 1920s, reaping huge profits directly and boosting the prosperity of other industries indirectly, such as factories that produced steel, rubber, and glass. In addition, other auto-related businesses also grew, such as gas stations, repair shops, used-car lots, motels, drive-in restaurants, and roadside advertising.

Automobiles affected the rural population even more. On the farm, a tractor or a truck was viewed as a necessity. Even during the Great Depression, truck ownership increased by 16 percent and tractor ownership by 70 percent between 1930 and 1940.

New cars await delivery at the Ford Motor Company. By the early 1920s, the automobile had become a necessity.

Overall, trucks and tractors improved production methods and provided transportation to market and the occasional trip to town.

Both rural and urban Americans enjoyed an increased awareness of the outside world with their new mobility. Rural residents in particular could drive to the city for purchases, see a movie, and meet people more easily. Road construction increased across the United States as a result, giving birth to the road construction industry today and related industries, such as cement, asphalt, and machinery manufacturers. Highways designed for faster speed were also rapidly built, shortening the distance between communities and increasing the mobility of Americans, including tourism.

Toward the end of the thirties, the automobile began to affect culture. People were no longer tied to the cities or needed to stay within a reasonable distance at work. Suburbia was born. Since the automobile made parental supervision difficult, dating and courtship also changed. Young people could escape the parental home and drive farther on a date. Parents began to exert less control over their children.

Newspapers

The newspaper industry was also transformed by technology. In the 1920s and 1930s, the daily newspaper grew from 27 million copies in 1920 to 41 million copies in 1940. Much of the growth can be attributed to the technology that improved the industry's efficiency. For instance, the teletype machine, a printing device used to send and receive telephonic messages, doubled the speed of the old telegraph. It was widely adopted in 1932 commercially and also used extensively by those in radio, aviation (for weather reports), and other enterprises.

As a further aid to newspaper efficiency, the wirephoto, soundphoto, and Acme telephoto perfected and increased the speed of sending pictures by wire between 1935 and 1936. Additional enhancement came with the Scanagraph in reproducing photos.

Telephones

Another technological breakthrough occurred in the area of telecommunications. The telephone had been rapidly changing the way Americans communicated ever since the early 1900s. But after World War I the technology entered a new stage of growth as newly developed industries across the country began demanding more telephone service. The telephone company spent much of the twenties extending its service area as a result, a period that also introduced the black rotary telephone and the panel switch in 1921, which allowed customers to dial locally without an operator for the first time. Another feature introduced was the party line, which largely increased telephone usage due to its cheaper cost. A party line was one telephone line shared by more than one household, which in 1929 comprised 63 percent of all residential phone lines.

In the end, all improvements decreased the connection time required to call long distance across country, which in 1920 averaged around seven minutes compared to one minute in 1928. On an international scale, transatlantic telephone service was initiated between New York and London in 1927 at seventy-five dollars per three minutes of conversation.

The telecommunications industry continued to make technological headway in the 1930s. In 1937 the underground coaxial cable and multiplexing made it possible for one cable to carry several long-distance calls at once. With the onset of World War II, telephone company engineers and inventors shifted gears to work on technology needed for the war, such as radio communication, microwave technology, and wireless communications.

Radio

Radio made its U.S. debut when KDKA of Pittsburgh, Pennsylvania, broadcasted the Harding-Cox election results on November 2, 1920. Between five hundred and one thousand listeners heard the broadcast that day, a "thrill never to be forgotten," Gleason L. Archer wrote in *History of Radio to 1926*, and an experience that "set in motion a movement that eventually encircled the globe."[3] But it was not until the end of 1921 when do-it-yourself radio kits became more available that radio gained popularity in the United States. Before long, hundreds of new stations and broadcasters joined the "radio boom," and by 1929 nearly 40 percent of all families in the United States owned a radio.

Like electricity, the telephone, and the automobile, radio helped decrease the isolation of rural America, but unlike any communication medium before, radio reached millions of people at once. People were instantly exposed to domestic and world news, politics, sports, and entertainment, receiving information faster than newspapers had ever provided. Listeners in the city

By 1929 nearly 40 percent of American families relied on the radio for news and entertainment.

and on the farm both could hear a variety of music, ranging from classical to jazz to Hawaiian. Humorous and drama-packed radio plays could be heard at the flick of the dial, along with morning exercise, Sunday sermons, auto repair instruction, baby care, and more, all serving to standardize or improve American speech and educate.

As popular as radio was during the 1920s, it soared to new heights during the 1930s. The depression actually lowered the price of radios in the United States, making more radios available to the population. Also, as the economy worsened, the radio was a welcome diversion from the financial concerns and daily woes of the depression. Between 1930 and 1932 alone, 4 million families purchased a radio, and by 1940, 86 percent of the population owned one. It was also during the period 1932 through 1939 that radio became a significant source of news in the United States, practically doubling the volume of news broadcasted.

Prior to the 1930s, the nation depended on newspapers for news, but radio made the news more immediate. Listeners could sometimes even hear an event as it took place, as in the dirigible airship crash of the *Hindenburg* in 1937. The announcer, hoping to report on the *Hindenburg*'s arrival in New Jersey, found himself reporting the fiery details of an explosion instead. Furthermore, radio had the advantage of allowing its audience to engage in other activities while listening, unlike readers of newspapers who required more concentration. Competition from the new technology would greatly affect the newspaper industry.

Radio was also the most persuasive advertising tool available in the 1930s. In addition to promoting products and services it was widely used by politicians. Without ever meeting the voters face to face, gifted politicians could inform and sway the population to their side. For example, during the depression President Franklin D. Roosevelt gave more than three hundred "fireside chats" on the radio, discussing foreign and domestic politics. Americans were overwhelmingly reassured by these chats and felt closer to the president as a result, often mailing fifty thousand letters a day to the White House following an airing. Robert J. Brown, in *Manipulating the Ether*, claims that "by the time of his death in April 1945, FDR had exploited the advantage of broadcasting so successfully that he was able to radically reshape the political, social, and economic structure of the nation."[4]

Radio was also widely used by British and French leaders and those in other European democracies. "By spanning the distance between the listener and the event, whether in New York, London, Berlin, or Tokyo, radio news greatly accelerated the process of tying the world closer together,"[5] Brown asserts.

The dictators of Europe also understood radio's exploitive potential in promoting their totalitarian regimes and took full advantage. For example, following Adolf Hitler's rise to power in 1933, Nazi propaganda was transmitted during broadcasts of music and plays and also over shortwave radio aimed as far as the United States. Radio use in Germany increased from 3 million to 12.5 million in the period 1932 to 1939. Hitler commented once that "without motor cars, sound films, and wireless [radio]"[6] his National Socialist Party would have failed.

Movies

Unlike radio, movies had been around since 1910. By the 1920s the motion picture industry was the fourth-largest industry in the country. In 1923 fifteen thousand silent film theaters existed across the nation. With the introduction of sound technology at the debut of *The Jazz Singer* in 1927, movie attendance changed overnight. In 1922 nearly 40 million people bought movie tickets on a weekly basis, but in 1929 there were close to 100 million.

Initially, the new sound technology was cumbersome for filmmakers. Few had mastered the sound equipment, and many were still in the process of converting their stages, as were the nation's theater owners. Cameras were noisy and microphones inadequate.

A technical refinement in 1929 that solved the noisy camera problem was a device called the camera blimp, which had a muffling effect. Filmmakers also learned to use a mechanical arm that held a microphone overhead. Eventually filmmakers learned to use sound artistically and productively, enabling them to make musicals and exciting films that attracted moviegoers. For example, gangster movies became more realistic with sounds of shooting.

Like radio and the automobile, movies also helped knit together a common community among Americans. On the screen viewers could observe the most fashionable clothes, hairstyles, tastes in food and drink, mannerisms, expressions, and even marriage or dating behavior. They could observe luxurious lifestyles, see exotic places, and fantasize about life unfamiliar to them.

Aviation

Aviation also underwent a huge transformation between 1920 and 1940, but progress was slow at first. As Walter Boyne notes, "Despite the great advances in aviation during World War I, aircraft were still like racehorses—delicate, given to indisposition and requiring endless personal attention from a host of technically qualified people."[7] Most pilots, or "barnstormers," in the 1920s were former World War I pilots. They led adventuresome lives, giving rides to the public, flying in air shows, operating flight schools, delivering mail, setting records in races, and serving as test pilots.

Meanwhile, independent aircraft builders began experimenting with new aircraft designs and learning to rely more on the science of aerodynamics and engineering. By the end of the 1920s some had become the first aircraft manufacturing companies. Commercial airlines also began operating, with less than 10,000 passengers by 1927, but more than 150,000 passengers by 1929. Some of the technological changes made included all-

The *Chicago*, built by Douglas Aircraft, completed the first around-the-world flight in 1924.

metal frames, cooling systems, added horsepower, advanced engines and propellers, and better piloting skills. All technological advances improved safety and increased the speed of travel.

According to Boyne, "By 1929, aviation had learned almost everything it needed to know to create the planes of the thirties."[8] Airplanes would soon become profitable.

Aircraft design advanced quickly during the 1930s, as demonstrated by the most successful plane developed in the history of aviation, the DC-3. Built by Douglas Aircraft Company in 1936, it made commercial transport profitable for the first time in aviation history as well as safer and faster. Moreover, the DC-3 was credited with the growth of the commercial airline industry worldwide.

Along this vein, similar growth in aviation was paralleled all around the world, but as World War II approached, Boyne remarks, "the greatest difference between the United States and other countries . . . was in American industrial capacity."[9] By the time World War II broke out in 1939, the United States was capable of building fifteen thousand planes a year. By 1944 its capacity would reach one hundred thousand, well exceeding Germany's capacity or Japan's.

Final Countdown

As the nation poised for war, America's industrial transformation had come to fruition. The aviation industry had matured and was receiving orders for airplanes from outside the United States. The spread of electricity during the twenties and the technological changes in automation and machinery during both the twenties and the thirties no doubt contributed to America's war success. Telephone technology (and radio) was primed to set up vital communications for the coming war and would eventually contribute to national security with the building of a submarine cable. Similarly, technology from the automobile industry would help build the jeeps and other vehicles used in the war. America's technological powers would not only help during the war but proceed at an even greater pace in the next decades.

Notes

1. David E. Kyvig, *Daily Life in the United States, 1920–1939: Decades of Promise and Pain.* Westport, CT: Greenwood Press, 2002, p. 58.
2. Frederick Lewis Allen, *Only Yesterday: An Informal History of the 1920s.* New York: Perennial, 2000, p. 56.
3. Gleason L. Archer, *History of Radio to 1926.* New York: American Historical Society, 1938, p. 204.
4. Robert J. Brown, *Manipulating the Ether: The Power of Broadcast Radio in Thirties America.* Jefferson, NC: McFarland, 1998, p. 9.
5. Brown, *Manipulating the Ether*, p. 110.
6. Quoted in Brown, *Manipulating the Ether*, p. 60.
7. Walter J. Boyne, *The Smithsonian Book of Flight.* New York: Random House, 1994, p. 115.
8. Boyne, *The Smithsonian Book of Flight*, p. 123.
9. Boyne, *The Smithsonian Book of Flight*, p. 167.

EVENT 1 **The Nineteenth Amendment Is Ratified: August 18, 1920**

Tennessee Legislation Locks in Suffrage for U.S. Women

by the *Literary Digest*

The long battle for woman suffrage in the United States ended in victory on August 18, 1920, with ratification of the Nineteenth Amendment by the Tennessee state legislature. Tennessee was the thirty-sixth state to give women the right to vote, satisfying the number of states required by Congress for the amendment to become law. In the following article excerpted from the *Literary Digest*, "The American Woman Voter Arrives," the author shares the nation's excitement and mixed response as news of the triumph quickly spreads across the land. Quoted are the reactions of prominent suffrage leaders, newspaper reporters, politicians, and even presidential candidates Warren Harding and James Cox, who will soon compete in the upcoming November election.

Whereas some see the Nineteenth Amendment as a victory for democracy and progress, others fear a loss of freedom in states' rights and potential harm to society. The antisuffragist publication *Woman Patriot* claims, "The suffragists are bringing us to the culmination of a decadence which has been steadily indicated by race suicide, divorce, break up of the home, and federalism." The publication's condemnation of the suffragists suggests the societal and

"The American Woman Voter Arrives," *Literary Digest*, vol. LXVI, August 28, 1920, pp. 9–11.

cultural obstacles that lay ahead for women and other minorities. More immediate obstacles involved state restrictions at voting polls and discriminatory laws preventing women from running for political office. But overall, women gained new status in society and added responsibility as citizens. The *New York Evening Post* speculates that many women are well qualified in their newly enfranchised role due to their participation in the suffrage movement. Still, the women have much to prove, and some observers wonder how their votes will affect the presidential election since the voting population, according to estimates, nearly doubled overnight.

In the end, women are credited with helping Republican Warren Harding win the presidency. After the amendment's passage, the antisuffragists encouraged women to vote against anyone who had supported suffrage. In Tennessee, for example, they succeeded in ousting the Democratic governor and placing Harding on the Republican ticket for president. Meanwhile, many Democrats presumed the suffragists would vote a straight Democratic ticket in the election out of gratitude for their support. However, in the final tally, the women voted similarly to the men, giving Harding one of the strongest popular vote victories in U.S. history.

The *Literary Digest* was published weekly by Funk and Wagnalls, publishers of dictionaries. The *Digest* ceased publication in 1938.

"Tennessee has triumphantly closed the sixty years of women's struggle for the right to have their prayers counted on Election day," says Mrs. Carrie Chapman Catt, president of the National Woman Suffrage Association. "Hell is going to break loose in Georgia if the Suffrage Amendment is ratified," predicted Speaker Walker, leader of the opposition in the Tennessee legislature; "this is now a white man's country and we have a white man's God." "American democracy, won for the white men by the Revolution, extended to all men by the Civil War, is completed by the woman's victory to-day throughout the United States," says Alice Paul, president of the National Woman's party. "Suffrage atavists have brought us toward the stage of squaw-rights reached five thousand years ago by the Hittites just before annihilation and by every other decaying civilization," declares *The Woman Patriot* (Washington, D.C.), an organ of the National Association Opposed to Woman

Suffrage. Thus speak leading friends and foes of votes for women, finally assured by the Tennessee legislature's ratification [on August 18] of the Nineteenth Amendment to the Constitution of the United States. By this amendment equal suffrage is extended to all the States [signed into law August 26, 1920] in time to vote this fall. Woman-suffrage organizations estimate the voting population as 26,883,566 women and 29,577,690 men; 17,500,000 women previously enfranchised by States, 9,500,000 more enfranchised by the amendment. State qualifications will affect actual exercise of the suffrage, and estimates of the woman vote at 20,000,000 or over may be excessive. But for the importance of its provisions, as the Newark *Ledger* observes, "the Nineteenth Amendment easily holds first place among formal changes made to this country's fundamental statutes." "The victory is not a victory for women alone," says the Kansas City *Star*, "it is a victory for democracy and the principle of equality upon which the nation was founded. As such it has an even greater meaning than the surface one most apparent. It means that our democracy is still in the process of growth, still capable of renewing its life and vigor and of adapting itself to the new requirements of a progressing age."

National political party leaders, the Presidential candidates, and President [Woodrow] Wilson responded to appeals for influence to secure ratification by the Tennessee legislature. After ratification Mr. [James] Cox said:

"The civilization of the world is saved. The mothers of America will stay the hand of war and repudiate those who trifle with a great principle. The action of the Tennesee legislature has another significance. It is an earnest of the Democratic policy to pay its platform obligations."

Senator [Warren] Harding said:

"All along I have wished for the completion of ratification, and have said so, and I am glad to have all the citizenship of the United States take part in the Presidential elections. The Republican party will welcome the response of American womanhood to its appeal to the confidence of all our people."

The Voting Population Doubles

Washington correspondents report that political managers are at sea concerning the probable alinements of new woman voters in the campaign. Claims of Republican and Democratic papers continue to follow the lines reviewed in *The Literary Digest* for August 7, based upon the records of the candidates; ratifications by Republican legislatures; the crucial thirty-sixth ratification coming from the Democratic South; the League of Nations being a divisive issue among women as among the men.

"Doubling the number of American voters will involve a transitional period of confusion, of readjustment," remarks the New York *Evening Mail*, which adds:

"The country may face it with a tranquillity born of the demonstration that in a field of related public activity women have proved a constructive force subject to no discount. As Red Cross nurses in the world-war, as munition-workers in the plants of the country, and as devoted and practical toilers in countless lines of war-activity, they performed a service that brought results and that had the very spirit of the men on the firing-line. The ballot crowns this service, and the service argues that the ballot will be well used."

Women Gain New Status

Says the New York *Evening Post:*

"Now that the battle is fought and won, there may be compensation found in the very fact that the contest was so prolonged and so arduous. It is better for the new women voters to have conquered the vote than to have had it bestowed upon them through easy acquiescence. The fight for suffrage has given the women an excellent preparation for citizenship. They are spared much of the painful apprenticeship in the methods and organization of political democracy. In a double sense the women voters have come into their own."

National League of Women Voters Is Formed

The National Woman's party will soon meet to determine its further activities. The suffrage victory means opportunity for more work and added responsibility, according to Mrs. Catt, who reports the formation of the National League of Women Voters by the National Suffrage Association. State branches are forming out of the old suffrage associations in the Pan-Partizan Educational League. "A woman can be a member of it and yet be a member of any political party she may choose, exactly as she may be a member of it and be a member of any church she may choose."

"Get into the parties" is the League slogan. Mrs. Catt says:

"In this hour of victory there is but one regret and that is that every man and woman in the nation does not share our joy. To-day there are those yet too blinded by prejudice to recognize the justice and inevitability of woman suffrage, but to-morrow we know that we shall work together for the common good of this great and glorious nation."

Opposition Continues

The antisuffragist point of view already quoted above is further detailed by *The Woman Patriot*, which says that ratification has been almost secured illegally and with very questionable methods because both parties put self-interest above public welfare. And—

"Decaying civilization of Canaanites and Jews and Polish partition came in an era of feminism. The suffragists are bringing us to the culmination of a decadence which has been steadily indicated by race suicide, divorce, break up of the home, and federalism, all of which conditions are found chiefly in primitive society. Antisuffragists have opposed rulership and force by women as contrary to human nature and stronger feelings, which demand specialization according to whether they are forceful, dominating, and machinelike, or whether they represent passive, intuitive, and the finer side of nature. It is the duty of antisuffragists to see that efforts to make double suffrage a complete success by transforming both sexes into weak neuters will be thwarted in educational channels so that this feminist disease which has already been contracted twelve times in the world's history will again subside. Because of women's greater love of deep instincts than of commercial careers and public competition with sons and husbands our fight has really just begun."

The fight against ratification in Tennessee raised the issue of State rights, because the State constitution prohibits the ratification of an amendment to the Constitution of the United States by a legislature whose members were elected previous to the passage by Congress of the resolution submitting the question to the separate States. The Nashville *Banner*, in Tennessee, holds that ratification is not final and means taking a case to the Federal Supreme Court. But the Baltimore *Sun* says:

"From the decided drift of the judicial mind, as indicated in recent decisions, there seems little hope from that quarter. What has happened in Tennessee is a *fait accompli*, and the Supreme Court has shown that it is inclined to side with the legions of success." . . .

In the South, where opposition to suffrage has centered, but which furnished the essential thirty-sixth State to ratify, the Richmond *Times-Dispatch* still criticizes enfranchisement by way of the Federal Constitution, but perforce accepts the situation, altho it adds a new and serious problem to control of the ballot-box in the South:

"It is not necessary to dwell upon that problem: every Southerner understands it thoroughly. However, a similar problem was boldly faced and boldly solved in the days following the Civil War. White supremacy was regained and maintained, and while conditions at times may become vexatious there need be no fear of any other than Anglo-Saxon domination."

Those in Support

The Louisville *Courier-Journal* calls the Tennessee suffrage action "a triumph which was inevitable, because the fight for it was a fight of reason, of justice, of civilization":

"Persons now alive will live long enough to look back upon the time when women were denied the ballot with something of the sense of detached wonder with which now we look back upon the time when human beings were denied their liberty, or the times when the world fancied itself at the zenith of progressive achievement without the telephone, the telegraph, or the steam-engine."

In the admission that suffrage by separate States is beaten, the Norfolk *Virginian-Pilot* says there is nothing of bitterness. It seemed that the principle of the right of each State to determine for itself the character of its electorate was worth asserting and defending. Nevertheless—

"If still another invasion of the State-rights principle is to be suffered, there is a degree of satisfaction in yielding this sovereignty in the cause of the enfranchisement of women. There is no argument against their participation in public affairs that is not to-day hopelessly archaic. . . .

"Far more pathetic is the case of the last-ditchers, who, indifferent to the merits of the State-rights issue involved, are oppressed with the fear that woman will pay dearly for her ballot in a coarsening presumed to be inseparable from participation in politics. . . .

"Woman was lovely in a bustle. She is no less lovely in puttees. We shall probably be as fatally in love with the golf-playing, candidate-scratching maidens of the years to come as our great-grandfathers were with the delicately pale ladies who knitted lavender samplers over their afternoon tea. Tastes in women change as surely as tastes in clothes."

Voting at the Polls and Possible State Restrictions

Constitutional phases of ratification are discust by the Washington *Star*, which points out that the Nineteenth Amendment simply removes a voting disability in a single respect:

"The women who by the removal of this disability are admitted to the polls must, of course, conform to other qualifications which may have been imposed by State laws. If this disability-removing amendment required confirmatory and enabling legislation by the States it would be subjected in effect to a dual ratification, the first as to form and the second as to effect.

"The Constitution does not in its provisions as to amendment require any double ratification. When a change is effected through the proposal of amendment by vote of two-thirds of the two houses of Congress and the ratification of three-fourths of the States, it is absolute. It may be evaded, as in the case of the Fourteenth and Fifteenth amendments, by the adoption by State legislatures of qualifying and restrictive laws, but such evasion is subject to correction by the Supreme Court."...

Overzealous Women

Several Northern papers, it may be noted, join in criticism of the suffragist tactics in Tennessee. They are "overzealous women," as proved by the unfavorable actions of the legislatures of Maryland, Delaware, and Louisiana, according to the Buffalo *Commercial*. The Albany *Knickerbocker Press* insists that "the bringing to bear of outside pressure upon lawmakers is an offense against government, and it is to blame for very many of our present-day evils. We should have less of it, and not more, if our Government is to be carried on with any permanence."...

Competing for Women's Votes

The Denver *Rocky Mountain News* goes into the reasons why Democratic party managers appealed to the South for final ratification:

"The South is opposed to woman suffrage because the economic urge of the North is only beginning to be felt there, and suffrage at bottom is economic just as slavery abolition was, just as prohibition was before it became part of the fundamental law.

"Democratic leaders have been anxious for ratification of the Amendment in time for November, as they seem to feel that with the 'solemn referendum' on the League of Nations and its appeal to women as a repressor of war as the party paramount issue, the woman vote may save that party as it did in 1916 in the enfranchised States on that other proposition of 'he kept us out of war.'

"If the Democratic party managers did not believe that the added woman vote would be to their good the South would not have saved the day for the Amendment. As an offset, Republican campaigners can point to the Republican States that months ago voted for ratification compared to the comparatively few Democratic States."

Women as Spellbinders and Civic School-Teachers

In lighter vein the Washington *Herald* calls upon us to consider some of the recent stages of woman's evolution in this country to the status of "spellbinders":

"First, she is a propagandist winning the right to vote. Next, she wins admission to the national political conventions as a speaker in behalf of candidates. Then she is accorded a place on the directing committees of the campaigns. Now she is to be given opportunity to speak with the men 'spellbinders' in the innumerable meetings to be held to convert voters. Meantime she is organizing classes to prepare both public and private 'workers' for the task of speaking most convincingly on issues of the campaign and on the merits of the candidates of both sexes.

"This last detail is significant. The civic school-teacher has arrived. The process of voting, due to woman's advent as voter and as candidate, is to be prepared for. Audiences that gather are to hear less rhetoric, flubdub, and bromidic stuff of a political and patriotic sort. Reason is to count for more than it used to, and emotion less. Tactics that men speakers used to employ in retorting to 'hecklers' won't go down.

"This will be sad news for a lot of professional stumpers of the male persuasion who were planning to use the old guile which men have fallen for for generations. They may draw their salaries from the national committees for the party 'sob stuff,' but they won't earn them—this autumn. 'Woman militant, woman pertinacious, and woman informed' will sit beside them on the platforms as speakers and in the seats as listeners. The citizen 'woman teacher' has arrived, and she will make many of the 'bunk' ladlers seem as ignorant as they really are."

What Suffrage Leaders Expect

Suffrage leaders expect the newly enfranchised women to use the vote to remove various State laws discriminating against their sex. There are, for instance, laws placing the custody of children exclusively in the hands of their father, and laws which, as now drawn, make women ineligible for office, and women who marry aliens lose their citizenship, and thus their vote.

EVENT 1 **The Nineteenth Amendment Is Ratified: August 18, 1920**

The Impact of the Nineteenth Amendment

by Nancy Woloch

The aftermath of the Nineteenth Amendment's ratification was not nearly as dramatic as the struggle before its birth. As author Nancy Woloch describes in the following excerpt, taken from her book *Women and the American Experience: A Concise History*, the suffragists entered the next phase with high hopes for the vote's impact on "political life, social reform, and women's status," and for a while, the political climate was promising. Woloch portrays the initial impact as impressive, a period in which it appears that women are well on their way to achieving political power. Twenty states quickly pass laws so women can serve on juries, and other states pass laws to protect women. In Congress the first federally funded health care act, the Sheppard Towner Act, passed in 1921, gave states matching federal funds to set up prenatal and child health care centers to assist expectant mothers and their children. Nevertheless, by the mid-1920s the reform effects of the Nineteenth Amendment were in rapid decline.

Woloch discusses the surprising behavior of women at the polls. Not only did they vote according to their husbands' political beliefs, but they also voted in fewer numbers proportionately. The expectations of suffragists and antisuffragists alike—that women would vote as a group ("in bloc") in a burst of "sweeping reform" to cleanse the world of its vices—never happened. Yet articles written

---

Nancy Woloch, *Women and the American Experience: A Concise History*. New York: McGraw-Hill Companies, Inc., 1996.

during this period declaring the failure of suffrage were more a symptom of the population as a whole, according to Woloch. She points out that voter turnout was down for both men and women. Only in isolated cases where black women were allowed to vote did the voting number of women match the men at the polls; however, state restrictions against blacks at the time kept their influence to a minimum.

Also noted with the passage of suffrage is the loss of a cause. Without a common denominator to rally around, the suffragists became divided among themselves, often between the older women of the movement and the younger generation, which appeared more interested in individual pursuits than women's causes. The women's movement was transitioning for sure, but perhaps more significant was the change occurring in society as a whole with the passage of the Nineteenth Amendment. Not only were attitudes between the sexes in obvious flux, changing the way that men and women interacted with each other and the world, but the merits of democracy itself also had been tested. By uniting as one for more than five decades and taking a stand, women had "achieved equality and independence."

Nancy Woloch is both an editor and a coauthor of American history books. She teaches history and American studies at Barnard College, Columbia University.

When [suffrage leader] Carrie Chapman Catt wrote her "inner story" of the suffrage movement in the 1920s, she itemized the unparalleled string of efforts that had been needed to attain the vote. Over the past half-century, suffragists had waged fifty-six referenda campaigns and hundreds of assaults on state legislatures, state party conventions, and state constitutional conventions, as well as on Congress. No other electoral reform, said Catt, had ever been so expensive or aroused such antipathy. In the aftermath of their triumph [in the passage of the Nineteenth Amendment], suffragists awaited the impact of the woman's vote on political life, social reform, and women's status. High expectations prevailed—on the part of both suffrage veterans, who envisioned the vote as a "first step," and the public.

Woman suffrage had an immediate impact. Polling places shifted from saloons and barber shops to schools and churches, to accommodate the newly enfranchised. Twenty states passed laws at once to enable women to serve on juries, and some states rushed through protective laws that women reformers had long demanded. Congress too seemed anxious to please women voters, at least for a few years. Its brief spurt of interest began with the Sheppard Towner Act of 1921, a plan to finance maternal education and child health-care programs, and ended in 1924 with passage of a federal child-labor amendment, which was never ratified. Throughout the decade, however, a Women's Joint Congressional Committee, representing major women's organizations, lobbied for passage of desired bills. And political parties at last began to cater to what was expected to be the "woman's vote." Both major parties welcomed women into their national committees. Finally, in a few localities (Chicago was one) there were signs that women did prefer the least corrupt and most reform-minded candidates and could influence the outcome of elections. But by mid-decade, it was clear that supporters and opponents of woman suffrage alike had overestimated the impact it would have on political life. The onus fell on the supporters. As [labor agitator and United Mine Workers organizer] Mother Jones once observed, suffragists expected that "kingdom come would follow the enfranchisement of women." During the 1920s, such millennial expectations—and even more modest ones—rapidly faded.

How Women Voted

A main false assumption apparently shared by suffragists and antisuffragists alike was that women would vote as a bloc. Or at least their rhetoric implied such an assumption. Over the decades, suffragists had often contended that women's votes would purify politics and end war, imperialism, disease, crime, vice, and injustice. According to antisuffragists, women as a group would be carried away by sweeping reforms and wives would vote against husbands, contributing to domestic discord, excessive individualism, social anarchy, and the collapse of the state. But none of the claims had immediate relevance. As the 1920s showed, women voted in smaller proportions than men. (Isolated data suggest that where blacks were permitted to vote, black women seized the ballot in the same numbers as black men and in greater proportions than white women; but limited by state restrictions and intimidation, black suffrage remained too small to affect elections.) Not only did women in general vote in smaller proportions than men, but they voted the same way as male relatives—of course, some antisuffragists had predicted this too. Unable to affect the outcome of elections, women never rallied behind "women's issues"—any more than they rallied behind women candidates, of whom there were few. "I know of no woman today who has any influence or political power because she is a woman," said Emily Blair, a Missouri suffragist who became vice president of the Democratic National Committee in 1924. "I know of no woman who has a following of other women." As politicians soon realized, there would be no great influx of women candidates or officeholders. Women did not seem to share political goals, they were unable to demand an array of reforms, and they voted as individuals, not as a bloc. Moral superiority, in short, had not carried over to the voting booth; the "woman's vote" did not exist.

The Decline of the Vote

Suffragists were not the only reformers ever to fall short of their own expectations. Other electoral reforms of the progressive era, such as the referendum, the recall, and direct primaries, historian William E. Chafe points out, also had little impact. Despite progressive efforts to democratize the electoral process, voter

Women cast their ballots for the first time following the passage of the Nineteenth Amendment in 1920.

turnout in the 1920s fell; only about half of eligible voters participated in presidential elections in the 1920s, for instance, compared to 80 percent in the late nineteenth century. Women alone could not be blamed for the decline, recent studies suggest, for male voter participation dropped as well. [Social worker and writer] Jane Addams made this point at the time: When asked in 1924 by the *Woman Citizen*, "Is woman suffrage failing?" she replied that the question should be "Is suffrage failing?" Still, women took the blame. By the mid-1920s, articles proclaimed the "failure" of woman suffrage, and veterans of the suffrage movement analyzed what had gone wrong. Women were disappointed in politics, contended Carrie Chapman Catt in 1923, "because they miss the exaltation, the thrill of expectancy, the vision which stimulated them in the suffrage campaign. . . . They find none of these appeals to their aspiration in the party of their choice." Emily Blair, in 1931, found deeper cause for disappointment. Feminism, said Blair, "expressed the desire of women once more to have a part in the making of the world."

> But it did not work out that way. The best man continued to win, and women, even the best, worked for and under him. Women were welcome to come in as workers but not as co-makers of the world. For all their numbers, they seldom rose to positions of responsibility or power. The few who did fitted into the system as they found it. All standards, all methods, all values, continued to be set by men.

Historian Chafe concludes that women "faced a no-win situation when it came to electoral politics." First, they had won the vote just when it declined in importance. Second, the two-party system, the lack of single-issue elections, and the varied class and ethnic interests of women voters precluded an independent women's constituency or bloc that could affect the existing parties.

The Loss of a Symbol and a Constituency

Lack of political clout was only one part of a double blow for suffrage veterans in the 1920s. It was compounded, as Carrie Chapman Catt suggested, by the loss of a cause. For decades, suffrage had served as a focus of feminist energies and a source of continuum between generations. "Hundreds of women gave the accumulated possibilities of an entire lifetime," Catt wrote in

1926. "It was a continuous, seemingly endless chain of activity. Young suffragists who helped forge the last links of the chain were not born when it began. Old feminists who forged the first links were dead when it ended." Some women had even personified the generational links—such as Harriot Stanton Blatch and Alice Stone Blackwell, daughters of suffrage leaders who both became leaders themselves. But once the umbrella of the cause vanished, the coalition of women that had gathered under it diminished and divided, often in factional disputes over protective laws and a newly proposed equal rights amendment. Indeed, the formation of the Woman's party in 1916 augured such disputes. Although organized women remained active throughout the 1920s, the inspiration of the suffrage campaign was difficult to recapture—or so its leaders suggested. "I am sorry for you young women who have to carry on the work in the next ten years," Anna Howard Shaw told Emily Blair, "for suffrage was a symbol and you have lost your symbol. There is nothing for women to rally around." Veteran suffragists especially regretted their inability to connect to the "rising generation," the post–World War I cohort of younger women, who took the vote for granted and lacked interest in women's causes. The new generation seemed to be carried away by a new sense of individualism, although not the sort that either suffragists or their foes had envisioned. . . .

What Contribution Did the Achievement of Woman Suffrage Make?

Neither miscalculations about the "woman's vote" nor the nature of women's politics after 1920 ultimately suffices to assess the achievement of the suffrage crusade. One question that remains is: What contribution did the achievement of woman suffrage make toward attaining the overhaul of attitudes demanded in 1848 and toward assaulting "aristocracy of sex"? Clearly, as Elizabeth Cady Stanton told her friend Theodore Tilton in the 1860s, lack of suffrage was a "symbol" of woman's degradation rather than a cause of it. Clearly, too, the achievement of woman suffrage redressed an inequity more than it bestowed political power. Its significance, however, can be suggested by turning to the elusive realm of attitudes as well as to the more concrete realm of involvement.

The first factor, attitude, was identified by Walter Lippmann in a *New Republic* article in 1915, when intense pressure for woman suffrage began to build. The vote itself would change nothing, Lippmann predicted, but the suffrage battle represented more than the gain of the vote. Rather, it represented "an infinitely greater change, a change in the initial prejudice with which men and women react towards each other and the world." As Lippmann observed, the change he was describing was almost "too subtle for expression." Women have to take part "in the wider affairs of life," he concluded. "Their demand for the vote expresses that aspiration. Their winning of the vote would be a sign that men were civilized enough to understand it." Historian Ellen Dubois suggests a related factor: She stresses the implications of women's involvement in the suffrage movement. Winning the vote, says Dubois, proved that women could unite to affect public policy and change the course of history, to serve as an active agency of change. "It was women's involvement in the movement, far more than the eventual enfranchisement of women that created the basis for new social relations between men and women," Dubois contends. The five-decade suffrage movement, she points out, actually accomplished the very goal that three generations of suffragists expected from the vote. By acting "deliberately and collectively," suffragists achieved equality and independence. The movement itself showed that "democratic participation in the life of the society was the key to women's emancipation," Dubois concludes. "Therein lay its feminist power and historical significance."

During the 1920s, women's organizations strove to maintain the collective spirit that had won the vote and to continue to act as an agency of change. But after World War I, new factors came into play. The new era was a politically conservative one, in which enthusiasm for reform dwindled and commitment to cause went out of style. The shift in political climate was accompanied by a major shift in social climate, one that had its most profound effect on middle-class women, the constituency of the woman's movement.

EVENT 2 The First General Assembly of the League of Nations: November 15, 1920

The League of Nations Meets for the First Time

by Giuseppe Motta

The League of Nations met for the first time in Geneva, Switzerland, on November 15, 1920. There, 241 delegates representing forty-one nations assembled to discuss a new means of conflict resolution in the world. Representing nearly every race, religion, and language on Earth, the League of Nations was the first world organization of its kind. In the following excerpt from *Living Age* magazine, Swiss president Giuseppe Motta gives the opening speech at the historic gathering. Noted absences at the assembly were Germany, Russia, and, in particular, the United States, whose nonattendance was keenly felt in light of the U.S. Senate's recent rejection of U.S. membership in the league and the failure of the league's creator, U.S. president Woodrow Wilson, to convince the Senate otherwise.

The League of Nations was originally part of Wilson's Fourteen Points peace proposal at the end of World War I. First presented to Congress in 1918, its purpose was to preserve international peace by guaranteeing the independence of nations through a collective pledge of support. Significantly, it would also ensure America's permanent participation in world affairs. At the Paris Peace Conference that followed in 1919, Wilson's League of Nations proposal was included with the Treaty of Versailles. However, Article 10 of the league's charter soon became a hotly disputed subject in the U.S. Senate, spearheaded by Republican senator Henry Cabot Lodge and isolationists (those resisting international involvement). Unwilling

Guiseppe Motta, "Welcome to the League of Nations," *The Living Age*, December 25, 1920, pp. 750–55.

to commit to the potential of war by promising the defense of other nations should future aggression arise, and concerned with territorial issues, the Senate rejected the Treaty of Versailles in March 1920, along with membership in the League of Nations. Wilson embarked on a campaign to overturn the Senate's decision, but he fell gravely ill before he could succeed.

Throughout the 1920s the league was successful in resolving a number of minor international conflicts and in establishing a world court. Nevertheless, during the 1930s it was unable to stop Italy's invasion of Ethiopia, avert the war in Bolivia and Paraguay, prevent Germany and Japan from pulling out of the league, or adequately handle the flood of Jewish refugees from Nazi Germany. Whether U.S. membership in the league could have averted World War II has been debated much over the years. Without the backing of the United States, the league was at an obvious disadvantage, yet it eventually provided a means to a new organization that the United States would fully embrace. In 1946 the League of Nations disbanded and the United Nations came into being, inheriting much of the league's structure and ideals already in place.

Giuseppe Motta was a Swiss politician, serving as president of the Swiss Confederation in 1915, 1920, 1927, 1932, and 1937. In addition to opening the first session of the assembly of the League of Nations, he was president of the assembly in 1924.

In the name of the Swiss people and the Swiss government, I, as president of the Confederation, welcome this eminent assembly, which convenes for the first time in the capital of the League of Nations. I shall not attempt to conceal the emotion which masters me in this historical moment, when I endeavor to measure in my thoughts the unprecedented significance and possibilities of what is now occurring on the soil of my own Fatherland. It is a great distinction which has been conferred upon my country, and I feel almost overwhelmed by the honor which has befallen me, in virtue of my office, of being first to welcome you in its name.

A Tribute to War-Scarred Belgium

My first duty on this great occasion is to express to the assembly our profound gratitude that Geneva has been chosen as the official home of the International Society which it is calling into life. We were fully aware that the choice lay undecided between Brussels and Geneva. If the selection had been determined exclusively by the glory of Belgium's recent history and late sacrifices, that noble nation's precedence could not have been denied. [Belgium was invaded by Germany at the start of World War I in 1914.] Belgium's coat-of-arms reflects the radiance of its moral greatness. In the same way that the heroic character of King Albert I will remain one of the most unsullied and purest in history, so will the fame of the Belgian people go down to posterity ennobled by their suffering. I fulfill a personally grateful as well as a solemn duty when, as the supreme magistrate of a government which remained neutral throughout the war, I declare that Belgium's loyalty to its international obligations, which it sealed with its own blood, will remain imprinted on the memory of men as long as the conception of right and justice endures.

Swiss Neutrality

I also wish to express the thanks of Switzerland to the Council of the League of Nations, whose distinguished members I have the honor to welcome. By its declaration at London on February 13, 1920, that Council made it possible for Switzerland to become a member of the League. The century-old neutrality of our Confederation was thus confirmed and made part of the permanent law of nations. For four centuries, Swiss policy has been guided by the ideal of neutrality. When the World War broke out in 1914, Switzerland did not hesitate. By remaining neutral my country believed it was complying with its international obligations and fulfilling its mission as a promoter of peace. A fortunate chain of circumstances which, in view of the smallness of the country and its location in the very center of the world's battlefield, borders on the miraculous, enabled us to preserve our neutrality to the end. Had the Swiss people been asked to surrender the armed neutrality which we justly consider our protection to-day as much as in the past, in order to join the League of Nations, we should have faced a painful choice between betraying our traditions and our historical mission or permanent exclusion from the new world order. The Council of the League undoubtedly consulted the wishes and the sympathies of our fellow nations in sparing Switzerland this painful choice. I trust that eminent body will appreciate the gratitude which we feel for this act.

A Message to America

Furthermore, I beg you, ladies and gentlemen, to send a cordial message of thanks and greeting to President [Woodrow] Wilson, who, as an act of spontaneous friendliness, has convened the first assembly of the League of Nations at its official home. With this message, I would couple an expression of the hope—or more than that, of the fervent wish—that the United States of America may not postpone longer taking its appropriate place in the League of Nations. A country blessed as is America by the bounty of nature, a glorious democracy which has also become a mighty melting pot of peoples, which it is fusing into a community of one language and one mind, a nation which is inspired by the highest idealism and stands in the forefront of material progress, a government which, through the weight of its wealth and its armies, decided the destiny of our hemisphere, a land which was the home of that hero of liberty, George Washington, and of that martyr to the brotherhood of man, Abraham Lincoln—that country, I say, cannot really close its heart to the call of its brother nations, which, retaining full possession of their independence and sovereignty, are uniting for common service in the cause of peace and the welfare of humanity.

Are the Fruits of War Adequate Compensation?

Unmeasurable, indeed, is the task which faces mankind in these hours of recovery from slaughter and ruin. We scan the pages of history in vain for a greater tragedy than that which we have experienced or witnessed. Even so tremendous an event as the slow decline of the Roman Empire seems but a shadow compared with the happenings of to-day. Never before have valor, self-sacrifice, patriotism, and military genius risen to equal heights. Heroism has exceeded every bound hitherto set by the human imagination and the records of history. In this sense, the war did, indeed, reveal the true greatness of man as both the master and the victim of nature. Never in previous history was the onslaught of armies so frightful. Never before in the records of the world were blood and tears shed so prodigally. Never before was the work of destruction pursued so ruthlessly and pitilessly. To be sure, the war was not solely a destroying agency. It helped people to achieve national unity, rectified old injustice, and broke many fetters. But was war the only way in which we might attain these ends? And are the good fruits we reap from the war adequate compensation for the ruin it wrought? There were certainly moments when every one of us asked himself whether the highest fruits of civilization—the sentiments of love, virtue and pity, the sense of justice, the consciousness of human brotherhood, and the inspiration of the finer arts—might not utterly disappear in the maelstrom of destruction.

The League's Foremost Duty

It was in this mood of the world mind that the ideal of a League of Nations seized with a force unknown before the hearts of all men who felt for their fellow men and whose unclouded spirit pierced the haze of prevailing passion. Experience had taught us that of all tragedies which can befall the race, war is the greatest—both for the victors and for the vanquished. Already there looms in the far horizon the shadow of coming conflicts, more deadly and more tragic even than the one from which we are emerging. We must, at any cost, make war impossible, or at least endeavor to minimize its horrors. That task naturally constitutes the first duty of a League of Nations.

The Beginning of a New Era

With respect and gratitude I do reverence to those benefactors of mankind, the philosophers and statesmen, the humanitarian idealists, the noble men and women who have championed the cause of a League of Nations in Church, in Parliament, in peace societies, and in international congresses; who have resolutely and persistently labored to transfer their vision from the realm of dreams to the realm of reality. I do reverence also to the uncounted multitude of mourning women whose eyes have been opened by the greatness of their sacrifice, whose resolve has been strengthened by consciousness of their newly won civic rights and duties; who, stretching their arms over the graves of the fallen, appeal to us for an era in which right shall be master over might. The hour which witnesses the coming of the League of Nations marks the beginning of an era which will permanently modify our forms of government. The obvious defects and inevitable inadequacies of the first League of Nations Covenant do not belittle this great truth. The work of the sower is never wholly unproductive. Even if the present structure were doomed to fall—forgive me if I suggest even this apparently impossible hypothesis—its foundations would remain and bid us build anew upon them.

Visions of a Great Human Family

Spiritual forces moved powerfully the millions of soldiers of every country who participated in the war. They sacrificed themselves on the altar of loyalty to their Fatherland; but in a larger sense, their sacrifice was to all humanity. Before their eyes hovered the vision of a great human family, from whose circle force and violence should be banished and among whose members unquestioned justice should rule. In the moment when that mysterious appeal from the realm of higher inspiration reached their ear, loyalty to their Fatherland was identified in their hearts with loyalty to mankind. I salute you, heroes of every nation, some crowned with glory, others unrecorded in the written scrolls of history—you, whom broad comprehension of your duty or instinctive intuition of right compelled; you, heroes, whose mortal remains lie under triumphal arches, in cathedrals, or in humbler graves in your own or foreign lands—I greet you all alike, with equal and unbounded tenderness, with an emotion which I do not attempt to master; for you are the divine seed of the harvest of the future—you are the heralds of a new era!

The Establishment of a World Court to Solve Controversies

Already it would seem an amazing thing to us did the League not exist. Yet it is folly to expect miracles. The individual is ever impatient, because his own days are but fleeting; but communities change solely because the period of their years is not numbered. Without the League of Nations, the treaties upon which peace has been based could not be applied. The powers of compulsion which the League possesses may be of doubtful value for many years to come; but already the League has the powerful moral backing of the conscience of the world. It may not be able invariably to avoid the use of arms, but it will enforce its authority mainly by higher means. If the first League of Nations assembly shall have created before it adjourns a permanent international court, it will have taken a long step forward toward the peaceful solution of controversies between governments.

The broader we make the basis of the League of Nations, the

surer the guaranties we shall erect for its authority, its impartiality, and its conciliatory influence. The victors cannot long dispense with the coöperation of the vanquished. It is a necessary condition for the existence of any league that all peoples shall march under its banner. Hatred is the mortal sin and curse of human society. Nations are never truly great unless they are great in forgiveness and in mercy. I should be false to my duty as spokesman of the Swiss people did I lack courage solemnly to affirm this truth to your assembly. Solidarity—moral, economic, financial—has survived even our era of destruction; it outlives the anger of nations, no matter how justified that anger may be. This first assembly will be called upon to consider the admission of new members, and will have the opportunity and the task of paving the way to make the League of Nations the world-embracing union which its ideal demands and which is imperative if it is to attain its object of assuring peace and eventual reconciliation. The day will come—I perceive it already in my own vision—when Russia, lifted from its present prostration of chaos and misery, will seek through the League of Nations the order, security, and aid necessary for its recovery.

The Lessons of the War

The League of Nations is not a league of governments. It is, as its name says, a union of peoples. For this reason, questions of disarmament, commerce, communications, hygiene, international finance, and above all, of labor, come prominently within its sphere of action. It is inconceivable that the nations of the world will henceforth tolerate the oppressive weight of their former military burdens. To do this would be to forget the lessons of the war. Governments will cease to erect high tariff walls against each other. All will have free access to the sea. Lands which produce raw materials, especially metals and fuel, will not try henceforth to monopolize their wealth. The financial conference at Brussels has made wise recommendations for restoring the vigor of our economic life. However, the gap between theory and practice is not so easily closed. Labor conditions are invariably governed by the laws of production, but they must also protect the worker's dignity as a man, and guarantee his sacred right to personal and domestic happiness.

Even a superficial observer must recognize that profound changes are occurring in the stratifaction of society. The fraternity of the trenches not only softened the bitter intellectual intolerance which formerly characterized the attitude of social classes toward each other, but it broke down the walls of petty pride between them; so that a new spirit pervades their relations in field and factory. In a halting and blundering way as yet, a new, enlarged democracy is taking over the reins of government. Political freedom is no longer merely an individual aspiration. It is a powerful motive in practical life, by which men are seeking to equalize the inequalities in their condition; although we realize that permanent and absolute equality is an ideal which—to our own salvation—we shall never attain. Democracy appeals to us as the best protection against violence, disorder, and the dictatorship of minorities. But it cannot perform its great tasks of educating and of governing peacefully the peoples of the world unless it guarantees to every individual unhampered opportunity to achieve his highest aims. In this quality, I might also say in this intellectual relationship, democratic institutions and the League of Nations are akin.

The League's Kinship with Democracy

However, we must not permit democracy to sink into the apathy of smug unvocal self-content. That kind of peace and order would be deceptive. That quiet would be the quiet of paralysis. Democracies are at their best when they are somewhat turbulent; for their very movements show that they are alive and acting. If they, for the moment, regard this new international order which we are establishing with some distrust, that but justifies our resting the greater hopes upon them. A century ago, the Holy Alliance hoped to check the progress of democracy; the League of Nations exists only by virtue of democracy. The oldest democracy in the world, the only democracy which insisted that its membership in the League of Nations should be decided by the direct vote of its citizens, extends through me its greetings to all other democracies, great and small, with a deep sense of our fraternity and our common mission. . . .

A Union Based upon Love and Solidarity

Permit me to express the wish that the deliberations of the Assembly may be ever governed by an effort at mutual understanding, and a spirit of friendly conciliation. The eyes of the world are upon you. I know you will not disappoint the hope which illumines their gaze. Permit me to conclude with the formula which we have inherited from our remote ancestors, and which closes every official communication between the Federal Parliament and the Swiss Cantons: 'We recommend you, loyal and beloved confederates, as well as ourselves, to the protection of God.' (*Wir empfehlen Euch, getreue, liebe Eidgenossen, mit uns dem Machtschutz Gottes.*)

The League of Nations will survive because it is a union based upon love and solidarity. Before this assembly of elected representatives of different civilizations, races, and tongues, in the presence of distinguished men who have come together from every quarter of the earth, of followers of every philosophy, and of the faithful of every religion, I commend the fortunes of the League of Nations to the protection of him whom Dante, in the glorious concluding verse of his divine poem, designates as the Love which moves the sun and the other planets: *'L'amor che muove il sole e l'altre sielle.'*

EVENT 3 **Benito Mussolini's March on Rome: October 31, 1922**

Mussolini Becomes Premier of Italy: An Eyewitness Account of the March on Rome

by Richard Washburn Child

In 1922 thirty-nine-year-old Benito Mussolini was leader of the Italian Fascists, a revolutionary body that was determined to create a totalitarian state. Since 1918 Mussolini and his black-shirted followers had been campaigning throughout Italy to convince the people that rule under fascism could solve the nation's economic woes and bring order to the political chaos. Italians grew enthusiastic over Mussolini's energetic speeches, embracing the Fascist slogans, the patriotic songs, and the flag waving that gave them voice and also empowered them against socialism and communism, concerns of many. As a result, Mussolini and the Black Shirts gained a following among the Italian people, who increasingly saw Mussolini's right-wing nationalist movement as the only means to restoring national order.

In late October 1922 Mussolini saw his advantage and threatened

---

Richard Washburn Child, "Open the Gates!" *The Saturday Evening Post*, vol. 5, July 12, 1924, p. 5.

to march on Rome. However, the king (Victor Emmanuel III) quickly averted a violent takeover of government and gave Mussolini control, granting him full dictatorial power. When Mussolini arrived in Rome to assume leadership as the youngest premier in Italian history, it was a hero's welcome. The fact that Italians were willing to overlook the Fascist Party's sometimes brutal and heavy-handed approach to law and order (a regime that would eventually be allied with Adolf Hitler's), speaks volumes on the epic hold that Mussolini had on the national spirit in 1922.

The following is an excerpt from Richard Washburn Child's 1924 article "Open the Gates," published in the *Saturday Evening Post.* As an American ambassador to Italy, Child was living in Rome with his family at the time of Mussolini's rise to power. His respect for Mussolini and the Italian people is apparent throughout his diary account of the famed takeover. Child's vivid detail of the streams of black-shirted Fascists marching into Rome provides insight into why Italians welcomed Mussolini's rule. Clearly, it aroused both pride and hopefulness, and although Child sensed the rise of a dictatorship, his assessment of Mussolini and the "Fascisti" neglected the darker side of fascism. Like many Italians at the time, it was one of admiration.

Though repressive and undemocratic, the Fascist regime never established a totalitarian state in Italy, nor did its leader become as ruthless as Germany's future dictator, Adolf Hitler. Nevertheless, the Fascist regime's downfall would begin with acts of aggression against Ethiopia and Spain, in 1935 and 1936, which cost the Italian taxpayers dearly, and equally important, their friendship with Britain and France. Mussolini's alliance (1936) with Adolf Hitler and subsequent role in World War II later cost Mussolini both his career and his life. He was executed in 1943.

Richard Washburn Child served as the American ambassador extraordinary and plenipotentiary to Italy under U.S. president Warren Harding from 1921 to 1924. He later assisted Benito Mussolini in writing his autobiography, *My Autobiography* (1928). Child held other government positions, served as a war correspondent, and practiced law, among other endeavors, but he is best known for his literary accomplishments as a popular writer of articles, short stories, and novels.

Rome, the Eternal City, so often taken, so often turned over to new control, through the ages, fell again and was entered by the Fascisti under our eyes.

One of the duties of an American ambassador is to observe with an unprejudiced vision, to report facts to his Government and, where possible, to prophesy coming events. My acquaintance with [Benito] Mussolini before he came into power had enabled me to perform these duties. . . .

I desire, at this moment, to report nothing but cold observation of an unparalleled revolution, which it was my privilege to see, but I cannot forget a day when, with a young Italian journalist, I was playing that I was not ambassador at all. We came out of a coffee shop and dangled our legs over the travertine wall, and this is what he said to me:

"Can't you sense it coming? Not like winter, but like spring?"

The Fascisti revolution came like that. All that year, and more every day, it was possible to sense the rise of national spirit. It had the inevitability of the approach of a new season. . . .

The Stirring of National Spirit

Yet, if one had stopped to listen, there could be heard the rhythm of universal desires and hungers on the march.

My two little girls, says my diary in October 1922, scarcely more than babies, having been playing in the Borghese Gardens, where Rome takes its children, came home and, putting aside feminine contempt for male attire, dug out of their wardrobe bloomers, which looked like Fascisti trousers, and created makeshifts for Fascisti uniforms. They went about all day singing the Fascista song, Giovanezza—"Youth! Youth! Springtime of beauty."

Mussolini had the whole country singing, and the song was not a song of battle and conflict, of class against class; it was a song of unity. And in those days if one turned away from the doctrinaires, the theorists and old preconceptions, one could sense the fact that Italy was falling into line—young men, titled idlers awakening to service, laborers who had gone down the dusty, sweaty trails of social reforms to nowhere, shopkeepers, men of the fields, the girls, their mothers, and even the children of foreigners on the benches in the Borghese Gardens.

The revolution in Italy—the stirring of national spirit against the drifting, the inactivity, the weakness of a government so democratic that it was always looted, and against talk and social theorists and sentimentalists—was also more than a revolution against anything; it was primarily a revolution for strong unity of purposes and strong leadership. . . .

It was raining in Naples on the twenty-fourth [at the opening of the Fascisti congress], but the populace, who stood on the streets in the rain, the military and naval attachés of foreign embassies and legations at Rome and the correspondents of the press saw in the parades of the Fascisti delegates, in their discipline, in the whole complexion of that assembly, some indication of a crystallization of the spirit of Italy, which might have given them food for hasty thought. I remember one of them—a military attaché, a general who had fought two fronts in the World War—said to me, "Well, I have seen them. That body of youth, the groups of the young women uniformed, the auxiliaries, the precision of movements! I would not have believed it possible; the world can well stop laughing at a machine like that."

I have often asked Mussolini what his thoughts were at the congress, so different from its unimpressive predecessor in Rome the year before. The membership of the Fascisti had now increased to more than three-quarters of a million; them had grown up a definite organization on military lines. Unlike organizations to which the ignorant sometimes compare it, there was nothing furtive or secret about it. It was the enemy of no race or creed. It was a sunlight organization, open to all who would join and accept discipline, and its nucleus was vigorous youth. Months before, I had written of the criticisms of the old Italian politicians who had said "Merely zealous boys"; I put down in my journal: "It is forgotten that this organization recruits those who are or will soon become new voters; it is like a young orchard which will still be bearing political fruit long after the old trees have felt the ax." . . .

Rumors of Opposition

History is, at best, a rickety structure of truth. Gossip and sensations sometimes crystallize into supposed truth. And yet it is worth while to recall the fact that one of the most reliable men from whom I received reports of what was going on came to me in that moment of Mussolini's decision, and told me in excited whispers:

"The march on Rome is now certain! It has been discovered that the socialist forces of the Left are planning a coup d'état.

There is to be a celebration at the Victor Emmanuel monument on the anniversary of our great victory in the war. Today a request was made for the use of the schoolhouses as barracks for the crowds who are coming into Rome. The Fascisti have discovered that the crowds, who were to be brought to Rome, would be armed forces of the Left. They would seize power and execute the Facisti leaders. You will see! Mussolini no longer has a choice. He must act at once."

Within a few hours after this report Mussolini had closed the congress in Naples, had rushed to the north of Italy, and the military directorate of the Fascisti had ordered mobilizations everywhere. . . .

Communication Lines Are Cut

News began to grow thin on the twenty-sixth and twenty-seventh of October. It was evident to one in Rome that telegraph, telephone and mail communication was being cut by the Fascisti. The mist of interrupted communication and censorship settled down over the Eternal City. It was like the thick walls of a heavy rain. The sky hung lower and lower. Before night of the twenty-seventh any dependable information of the state of affairs from beyond the walls of the city was almost impossible to obtain.

The government had ordered the cutting of railroad lines. Late that night word was brought to me that army trucks were taking barbed wire to the outer defenses of the city and that the gates were being closed and fortified; there was tension, but the government was secretive, the press was mild. Dinner parties went gayly forward. Civil war was on its way with a menace of blood on the old cobblestones, but Rome appeared as a philosophical personality awaiting almost everything with a shrug of her shoulders.

Troop Movement Throughout the Night

That night I heard down in the old Piazza Montenara the shuff-shuff of the feet of infantry. Dark phalanxes of fighting men were moving through the rain.

My diary for the next day, October twenty-eighth, recalls to me vividly that period of tensity:

"All through the night there were the usual signs of troop movements—distant bugles and the rumble of army trucks. At breakfast we learned through the newspapers and from reports over the telephone that night had brought forth many developments. Rome, so often marched upon and besieged, was again cut off and surrounded and under martial law.

"We have full confirmation that the Fascisti action has been nation-wide. . . .

"Rain! Rain, wind-whipped and gray, was flying across the great almost empty Piazza Venezia as I went off to the embassy offices. A line of autobusses, evidently commandeered to move troops in emergency, stood dejected below the palace wall, and out in the middle of the square, under soldier guard, were covered army lorries with canvas flapping about, concealing, no doubt, machine guns. The streets were almost deserted; they were heavy with a depression and emptiness like those of a city whose population has been taken off by a sweeping plague. A traffic guard who stopped my car told us that the trams had been stopped and the movement of all motors had been forbidden. My chauffeur explained that I was the American ambassador. The guard motioned us to go on. A group of dripping Fascisti in black shirts and steel helmets came forward into the street, perhaps with the idea of commandeering my car. They returned, disappointed, to the doorway of one of the close-shuttered shops. Like other groups, they appeared to be waiting to give aid from within the city if their brothers, who marched upon it from without, met resistance.

"The army's cavalry stands in side streets awaiting orders. The horses' patient heads are down after a night in the rain. Auto trucks filled with infantry, cough, explode their exhausts and roar along over the cobbles. Barbed wire moves along in trucks, shiny and new. Behind the entrance to the courtyards of government buildings squads of *carabinieri* [military police] and soldiers of the regular army hang on their bayoneted guns. . . .

"During the morning a proclamation of siege and martial law was posted on the buildings along the streets. It is said to bear the signatures of the ministry who have presented resignations to the King and been asked to remain in office. It forbids assembly, enforces a curfew, prohibits the circulation of all vehicles. It is regarded as a declaration of war. . . .

"Evening. The King has evidently changed his mind. He must have acted soon after midday. He announces that he did not sign the decree declaring a state of siege and that he will not do so. All the rules issued by the military command have been relaxed and the decrees are being torn down. News from outside Rome is that the advancing Fascisti squadrons have captured various stores, machine guns and field pieces, and have many more motor cars and trucks."...

The King Sends for Mussolini

"The King has sent for Mussolini. Already the military and city authorities are planning to receive the hordes of invaders. The tracks, torn up to cut railway communication, are being relaid, and it is reported a special train is bringing Mussolini, whose name now appears in capitals and who is called *Duce*—Leader."...

Rome Opens Its Gates to Mussolini and the Fascisti

"I motored about to see if there were substantial disorder, but I could find none. Motor cars loaded to the running board with black shirts come steaming out of the muddy approaches to Rome. Girls on balconies cheer them. The Italian flag is everywhere. As the rain has thinned down, the people come out and there is no sign among them of opposition or resentment; on the contrary there is an atmosphere of welcome and joy. A small crowd in front of the Quirinal [King's residence] cheers the King."...

The next day, Monday, I stood in my window in the embassy offices watching the columns of the invaders passing from the railroad station or coming from the Via Nomentana. It was a muddy, tired, healthy lot. And very happy.

They came by in an eternal marching stream, hurtling forward in the unconventional ground-getting gait of the Italian countryside. Some wore uniforms, some wore long, wet, working men's trousers with the black shirt tucked in at the belt. Some companies were equipped with full uniforms—steel helmet or tasseled fez, short trousers, putties—lean and businesslike as black hornets. Some detachments dragged machine guns. Some were fully equipped with rifles.

I could see old men who had been on the march across the open Campagna for two days, hungry, wet, sleepless. Their eyes were bright; they had entered Rome. Some men carried shotguns, some only heavy walking sticks. All day long there was the shuff-shuff of marching feet coming out of the night and the rain. . . .

I could not believe what I saw; I saw the entry into a great city of nearly a hundred thousand men of all classes of life; some without education, some used to the roughness of mountains, of dockyards, of industrial warfare, all of them victors in the taking of a prize, and yet subjecting themselves to discipline. Many of them—indeed most of them—were alive with the fires of youth; and they restrained these fires. . . .

My diary on October thirty-first says:

"Mussolini has formed his ministry. He will occupy the premiership—the presidency of the Council of Ministers. He will take temporarily, it is understood, the portfolio of Minister of Foreign Affairs. This causes some of my diplomatic colleagues great alarm, for they say he will be a firebrand in the European situation. The newspapers announce that he will also be Minister of the Interior. The term dictator was first applied to Mussolini this morning. . . .

"By daylight the plans for a great victory parade of the Fascisti were under way!" . . .

I watched that parade with my wife, in that enjoyable advantage an ambassador can sometimes seize of being one of the jostling crowd. We went out to see it at four o'clock in the gray afternoon. It had been marching since one.

A few hours had allowed the Fascisti to brush up a little; the mud was knocked off, uniforms adjusted, or acquired, columns were straightened out, and officers who had snatched a little sleep could give commands with more snap. It was youth and the spirit of the crusaders that came swinging down the Corso toward us in the Piazza Venezia. They came with the swinging glad melody, Giovanezza, which was thrown back at them from the crowd, was echoed between buildings and filled the open piazza over the soil which once had felt the rumble of the triumphal cars of the Caesars.

Column after column came up to the steps below the tomb of the Unknown Soldier and presented their tribute with the salute of the Roman Republic revived by the Fascisti. This is a throwing forward of one straight arm in the direction in which the salute is to go—palm of the hand down; it is gesture suggesting equally welcome or farewell, democracy or benediction. Then as the brass bands crashed out a new march and the tricolor of Italy streamed forth into the wind, the same columns went singing away to the palace, where the King, on the balcony, in his army uniform, saluted and acknowledged their cheers.

There were companies of women Fascisti too, springy of step, black waists, marching with vivacity but wearing a dignity on their faces. There were young girls, laughing. But in the main the composite face of that parade was the brown lean face of sinewy Italian youth. It was a face which has been seen before; it was the face of Garibaldi's Thousand. [In 1860 Giuseppe Garibaldi captured Sicily in an attempt to unite Italy.] There was nothing soft about it. It was happy and its eyes shone, but it was a face of stern vigor. . . .

"They Call Me a Dictator"

And yet as I stood in the Piazza Venezia with the swing of marching youth before my eyes, I confess that my thoughts went away from that pageant and that I no longer for a moment heard the marching song flung up by band and human voices.

I began to think of Mussolini. I began to think of him as he had said farewell to me only a few days before, when unattended, he walked out of the Orsini Palace and turned to wave his hand to me. I began to wonder if he were now standing somewhere with his head erect with pride of power or was looking at the ground thinking as I was thinking that an almost impossible task confronted him.

He could contemplate, if he would, the utter chaos and the stifling rubbish of a misguided democracy, run wild. He could contemplate a people sapped of men and resources as no other of the victors of the war. He could contemplate the immutable economic facts. He could face the realities of disordered finance. He could foresee the difficulty of restraining mad impulse and of prodding dull sloth. He could foresee conspiracy, opposition and the need for an iron hand. He could foresee treachery among friends, lies among enemies. He could foresee the multitudinous details and the immovable bulks in the way of building a new state—a new Italy.

He must have thought of these things, because when he came to see me two days later as Premier of Italy he said to me, "They call me a dictator. Already the foreign press is heaping abuse on me. But I do not know where in all the world there is another man who would take the job I have before me."

E V E N T **4** **Charles Lindbergh Makes the First Transatlantic Flight: May 21, 1927**

Lindbergh's Unforgettable Flight

by *Outlook*

In May 1927 a number of pilots entered a flying contest in the United States to pioneer a nonstop transatlantic flight from New York to Paris that would capture a prize of twenty-five thousand dollars. Charles Lindbergh (1902–1974), a hopeful young airmail pilot, accepted the challenge and took off alone across the Atlantic in a single-engine monoplane christened the *Spirit of St. Louis*—a plane that had taken less than two months to build. Hampered by low telephone wires at takeoff, ice on the wings during flight, and a lack of sleep the night before, Lindbergh managed the journey in just over thirty-three hours, achieving the first nonstop solo transatlantic flight ever made. The world immediately showered him with praise and recognition. According to the following *Outlook* magazine article, it was as if Lindbergh had "fired the imagination of mankind . . . had evoked all that was best in men's hearts and minds."

According to *Outlook*, thousands of shouting Parisians greeted Lindbergh at the French airport. "Well, I did it," remarked the overwhelmed pilot, both embarrassed and astonished by his unexpected fame. In fact, he had expected few to know him, having prepared six letters of introduction in advance just in case. Instead, the French received Lindbergh with honors befitting a "ruling monarch or president." Lindbergh returned the honor by paying tribute in a

"An American Viking of the Air," *The Outlook*, vol. 146, June 1, 1927, pp. 139–40.

speech to two missing French pilots who had failed to complete their own transatlantic flights, further demonstrating his humility and genuine manner that apparently impressed all he met.

Lindbergh's flight itself was an extraordinary feat of cooperation between man and machine, according to *Outlook.* For instance, he did not have a navigator on board for the sole purpose of saving weight; instead, he relied on an inductor compass and the earth's magnetic force. The two crude methods of navigation amazingly permitted him to arrive within three miles of Ireland. To enhance his visibility, Lindbergh used a periscope and two side windows. At one point, weather nearly destroyed the *Spirit of St. Louis* when ice built up on the wings, dragging the plane down to just ten feet above the water.

Outlook was a weekly magazine published from 1923 to 1928.

Charles Lindbergh, twenty-five years old, American, climbed out of his airplane on Le Bourget flying field near Paris. A score of men lifted him and let him down to the ground. A multitude, numbering thousands, encircled him.

"Well," he said, "I did it."

Did what?

He had no idea of what he had done.

He thought he had simply flown alone from New York to Paris. What he had really done was something far greater. He had fired the imagination of mankind, he had evoked all that was best in men's hearts and minds, he had erased rancor and suspicion and had lighted a flame of good will, he had started a clean breeze around the world, he had somehow imparted to his fellow-men, without respect of race or nation, a new vigor.

What this young air-mail pilot has accomplished no one could have foreseen.

Instant Recognition and Praise Worldwide

He, least of all, anticipated the effect of his flight. He started out with a razor, a toothbrush, a passport, and six letters of introduction in his pocket. Apparently he thought that when he arrived he would need to clean up, have a shave, and then start out to make some acquaintances in a land of strangers. Those things that he carried in his pocket were symbols of his achievement. This fellow, who has been received in France with honors usually reserved for a ruling monarch or president, who has received an acclaim from the world like that enjoyed by few men in history, has won his greatest triumph just because he never once thought of it.

If there had been any element of braggadocio, of false pretense, of self-seeking, of vanity, in Charles Lindbergh he couldn't have done what he did. He might have flown to Paris and won the $25,000 of the Orteig prize for the first flight to that city from New York; but he could never have stirred the world into admiration. "We could have gone a thousand miles more," he said, "—or at least five hundred." "What do you mean by 'we'?" he was asked. "Well, you know," he answered, "the ship was with me." He has been nicknamed "Lucky." He deprecates the term. Luck, he declares, is not enough. Does he mention daring? or skill? or intelligence? No. It is his plane, and engine, and instruments.

Charles Lindbergh is the heir of all that we like to think is best in America. He is of the stuff out of which have been made the pioneers that opened up the wilderness, first on the Atlantic coast, and then in our great West. His are the qualities which we, as a people, must nourish. They are certainly the qualities that win, throughout the world, instant recognition and praise. . . .

Lindbergh's Tribute to Two French Airmen

In the glory of this triumph not the least share belongs to the French people. Their generous reception of the American aviator while the grief over the loss of their own transatlantic flyers, [Charles] Nungesser and [François] Coli, was fresh, is the surest evidence of French character. If the victor in this competition had been one of themselves, his reception could not well have been more glorious. And Charles Lindbergh showed that the tribute that they gave him was deserved; for the first visit he made in Paris was to the mother of Nungesser. Moreover, in his first speech to the Aero Club, he paid tribute to Nungesser and Coli in which he said that their heroic effort "was a far greater project than the one completed Saturday night." And he expressed the hope that "the brave French airmen may yet be found.". . .

How the Flight Began

The flight that ended at Le Bourget began almost unheralded. It had been known that a young airmail pilot had entered as a competitor for the prize of $25,000 which had been offered by Raymond Orteig, a New York hotel man of French nativity. Others were preparing for the transatlantic flight. The Bellanca plane was tuning up on Long Island and was the chief center of interest. Almost without warning, young Lindbergh came from San Diego, California. He stopped only once on his transcontinental flight. That was at St. Louis. He had scarcely arrived in New York before he seemed ready to start again eastward. Then, early one morning, he was up, went out to his plane, and as soon as his fuel tank was filled started on his transatlantic flight.

The Flight

In his cramped cockpit he faced his fuel tank and instrument board. All that he could see ahead was through a periscope. On each side of him was a window. Down below him was an opening through which he could look to learn of what is known as the

Charles Lindbergh (left of center) completed his historic transatlantic flight in just over thirty-three hours.

drift of his machine. He had no navigator with him. He said he preferred to save the weight. Perhaps also he preferred to save possibilities of a difference of opinion on the way. At any rate, he took an inductor compass. This is an instrument, American made, which sets up an electrical field that holds an indicator in constant relationship with the magnetic lines of force on the earth. Thanks to this instrument, Lindbergh arrived over Ireland within three miles of his objective. On the way he encountered a sleet storm that threatened to cover the wings of his plane with ice and drag him down; but his skill and courage enabled him to fly out of trouble. He swept from ten feet above the water to ten thousand feet, seeking a level where the sleet was not. At last he saw the Seine [River], then the lights of Paris, then the flying field, and then the shouting, overwhelming multitude.

Where Next?

Now he wears the decoration of the Legion of Honor and is threatened with a medal from Congress. He apparently can have any job he wants from vaudeville up or down. But he says he wants to get back to the airmail service—if they will take him.

E V E N T **4** **Charles Lindbergh Makes the First Transatlantic Flight: May 21, 1927**

The Legacy of Lindbergh's Flight

by Tom D. Crouch

Charles Lindbergh's 1927 solo flight across the Atlantic would change his world forever, having both a positive and a negative effect on his personal and public life. Following his record-breaking flight, immediate honor and recognition abounded, which included the U.S. Congressional Medal and opportunities to retell his story to the press and in his own words. There were also enticing offers to endorse certain products, such as cigarettes or automobiles, which he politely declined because his real desire was to promote the safety of flying. That same year he applied his skill at Pan Am Airlines as a technical adviser, an expertise that eventually benefited other airlines and aircraft manufacturers. The world watched with interest as their favorite celebrity developed his career and public life and later his personal life, when he married Anne Morrow, the daughter of an American ambassador. Tragically, in 1932 the couple's child was kidnapped and murdered. As the world mourned and awaited details, the overwhelmed couple fled to Europe to seek refuge from the press. From there, Lindbergh's undeniable mark on the world persisted until his death in 1974. His achievements in aviation history are commemorated to this day, and his story continues to inspire all who hear it.

In the following selection author Tom D. Crouch speculates on the reasons behind Lindbergh's long-lived fame and the continued interest today in his achievements. Part of the reason, Crouch suggests, is the tremendous impact he made on his own decade. By 1927 the postwar period had already given birth to civil war, eco-

---

Tom D. Crouch, "Lindbergh: An American Hero," *Air & Space*, Summer 1981, pp. 3–4.

nomic unrest, political turmoil, and three major dictators—Benito Mussolini, Adolf Hitler, and Joseph Stalin. Lindbergh could not have timed his flight more perfectly. As the only pilot to fly solo in the transatlantic flight contest (others had flown in teams), and as one who chose not to brag about his accomplishment, Lindbergh came to represent the ideals of courage, traditional values, youth, and the pioneer spirit.

Crouch's description of Lindbergh's contribution to the aviation industry and to other nonaviation areas provides concrete evidence of Lindbergh's lasting influence. Some examples noted are his mapping of air routes later used by passenger airlines, his support of rocket experimentation, his help during World War II, his contribution to the medical field, and his work in saving wilderness areas and endangered species. Lindbergh won the Pulitzer Prize in 1953 for his autobiography, *The Spirit of St. Louis.*

Author Tom D. Crouch has been curator of aeronautics at the Smithsonian Institution's National Air and Space Museum in Washington, D.C., since 1974. He is known for his works on the history of aeronautics and has received a number of book awards, such as the Christopher Award in 1990 for *The Bishop Boys: A Life of Wilbur and Orville Wright* and the Aerospace Writers Association Literary Award in 1980 for *"Apollo": Ten Years Since Tranquility Base.*

Millions of visitors make the pilgrimage to the Smithsonian Institution each year, drawn by a desire to see for themselves the priceless bits and pieces of their national heritage. They gaze at the Star Spangled Banner that Francis Scott Key saw still flying over the walls of Fort McHenry in the dawn's early light. They stroll past canvasses by Rembrandt, Picasso, Peale, and West; admire gowns worn by first ladies from Martha Washington to Nancy Reagan; and wonder at the fragility of the wooden boat that carried John Wesley Powell through the rapids of the Colorado River.

But for many of these visitors, the high point of the tour arrives when they walk through the doors of the National Air and Space Museum and see a small silver monoplane hanging overhead. In a museum filled with the most famous vehicles in the history of flight, from the world's first airplane to the Command Module that carried our first astronauts to the Moon, the *Spirit of St. Louis* retains its special significance.

For a people who have great difficulty distinguishing mere celebrity from genuine heroism, our continued interest in Charles A. Lindbergh and his achievement seems to require some explanation. This is particularly true when we realize that many of those visitors who instantly recognize the *Spirit of St. Louis* have only a hazy notion as to what Lindbergh accomplished. (He was the first to fly the Atlantic, wasn't he?) We are left with a question. Why do we remember, even revere, Charles Lindbergh long after other pilots and aircraft that made great flights have been forgotten?

Part of the answer lies in the enormous impact Lindbergh made on his own time. Few events in the history of aviation have so electrified the Nation and the world as did Lindbergh's solo transatlantic flight of 1927.

Lindbergh as a Symbol of Traditional Values

On the most obvious level, the flight was a demonstration of the maturity of aeronautical technology, forecasting the day when scheduled transatlantic air service would become a reality. However, it was the public perception of the Lindbergh personality that was to lend symbolic significance to the event. Jazz-Age Americans refused to view the flight as a simple triumph of technology over time and space. Rather, Lindbergh's achievement was seen as a reaffirmation of the importance of traditional values that seemed increasingly vulnerable in a more complex and mechanized world.

Charles Lindbergh could hardly have chosen a more auspicious moment to make his appearance on the American scene. The Twenties had been a decade in search of a hero. Unlike other celebrities of the period, Lindbergh performed, not within the artificial restrictions of the playing field or on the movie lot, but on the limitless stage of the sky. Other pilots seeking to capture the $25,000 Orteig Prize had adopted a team approach. Many had chosen to fly large multi-engine aircraft that seemed to offer some measure of safety and comfort. Charles Nungesser, François Coli, Noel Davis, Stanton Wooster, Richard Byrd, and Rene Fonck had all tried and failed. Stories of the death and injury of would-be transatlantic aviators had filled newspaper headlines for weeks.

Lindbergh appeared suddenly, setting cross-country speed records as he flew from San Diego to St. Louis, then on to New

York. His airplane, a small single-engine monoplane, had been constructed by Ryan Airlines, a relatively unknown firm, in only 60 days.

Lindbergh dared to begin his journey while others waited for a break in the foul weather over the North Atlantic. The takeoff, a series of bounces off muddy Roosevelt Field, came on May 20, 1927, and seemed calculated to impress spectators with the dangers inherent in the enterprise. Then he was gone, flying alone while a world waited in suspense. From the moment the *Spirit of St. Louis* touched down at Le Bourget [airfield near Paris], the millions who searched for ideals and stability in an age of confusion and anxiety adopted Lindbergh as their own.

Writing in *Popular Aviation* in 1928, pilot Margery Brown focused on Lindbergh as the personification of traditional virtues in explaining the wave of enthusiasm and adulation that followed the flight:

> Lindbergh is a symbol, more or less. It isn't Lindbergh the person who inspires them so much as it is Lindbergh as an ideal. They recognize in him qualities they would like to possess—courage, quiet confidence, modesty, and spiritual freedom.

Lindbergh as a Role Model

The young aviator was cited as an example of the success that would come to those who attacked their problems with courage, confidence, and perseverance. The 18-year-old editor of the San Marcos College student newspaper, Lyndon Baines Johnson, was one of many who saw Lindbergh as the ideal role model for young Americans:

> Lucky Lindy is the hero of the hour, yet the adjective which most characteristically describes Lindbergh is not lucky, but plucky. . . . A sketch of his life reveals the grit and determination that have been outstanding traits of his. . . . He is a simple, straight-forward, plucky lad whose first lesson learned was self mastery. He did not give up when hardship and trials beset him. . . . His pluck carried him through to success and fame. . . . It is a wonderful thing to make the first trans-ocean flight and achieve spiritual independence. Still more wonderful is the fact that this feat lies within the grasp of all of us. Students, the choice lies with you. Do not sigh for Lindbergh's wonderful luck, but determine to emulate Lindy's glorious pluck.

Clearly, the public perceived Lindbergh as a larger-than-life figure, a latter day folk hero. He was a modern frontiersman who pitted himself and his airplane against the forces of nature in much the same fashion as Daniel Boone had challenged the Kentucky wilderness a century and a half before. It seemed entirely appropriate to include Lindbergh's profile along with those of Boone, [George] Washington, and [Abraham] Lincoln on the cover of the *Boy Scout Handbook* in use during the 1930s.

His Impact on Aviation

Catapulted to sudden fame, Lindbergh was to remain a public figure until his death in 1974. Through his activity as a consultant for a number of airlines and aircraft manufacturers, he left the indelible stamp of his personality on the growing aviation industry. The long distance flights that he undertook with his wife, Anne Morrow Lindbergh, pioneered routes that would one day be followed by passenger airlines. His interest and support of the early rocket experiments of Robert H. Goddard forced a doubting public to take note of the possibility of travel beyond the atmosphere. During World War II, Lindbergh worked for the improvement of military aircraft and drew on his own vast experience and superb piloting skills to teach young aviators how to wring the last ounce of performance from their aircraft. During his tour of U.S. bases in the Pacific, he flew a number of unofficial combat missions himself, and is credited with the destruction of at least one enemy airplane.

But Lindbergh's interests were far too broad, his talents too enormous, to remain limited to aeronautics. As he himself was to comment:

> When I look back on the early years, I realize it was the art of flying more than its science that intrigued me—it was the combination of an underdeveloped science with an art, resulting in adventure for the mind and body that brought stimulation to the spirit. As the science has developed, the art and adventure have declined—and with them, my interest.

Influence Beyond Aviation

During the 1930s he worked with Dr. Alexis Carrell of the Rockefeller Institute to develop a perfusion pump that would serve as a first step toward the creation of a heart-lung machine. His enormous prestige and knowledge of military affairs led to his rise as an influential, and not always popular, commentator on domestic and foreign affairs prior to 1941.

With the coming of peace he continued as a consultant to various military agencies, devoting long hours to the maintenance of U.S. aerospace leadership. During the post-war years, however, his attention was increasingly focused on problems of central concern to a world beset by environmental woes. He worked to save wilderness areas and to preserve vanishing animal species. He was particularly concerned with the plight of primitive tribes struggling for an accommodation with the modern world.

May 20–21, 1981, will mark the 54th anniversary of the first solo transatlantic flight. In observing the occasion, we will be commemorating far more than the flight of the *Spirit of St. Louis;* we will be honoring the career of Charles Augustus Lindbergh, the man who, more than any other, has come to symbolize the daring, skill, and judgment that have opened the heavens to mankind.

EVENT 5 **The First Talking Motion Picture, *The Jazz Singer*, Debuts: October 6, 1927**

The Jazz Singer Marks the End of Silent Film

by Robert E. Sherwood

Warner Brothers Pictures acquired the Vitaphone in 1926, a device that synchronized sound on disc with a movie projector and allowed for the first time actors to speak in films. Warner Brothers had no idea whether it would prove successful. The venture was a gamble. Warner Brothers was heavily in debt, and although the advent of sound in the moving picture industry seemed inevitable, the timing was debatable. Many major movie studios were still hesitant to make the transition from silent screen. The financial risk concerning audience acceptance, the investment required in new equipment, and the obvious pressure on silent stars and directors to evolve seemed too major a risk, so most studios approached the idea with caution.

Added to this, synchronized sound (researched for years by various entrepreneurs and scientists) remained crude in quality. Voices and other sounds were irritating (scratchy) to the ear. However, Warner Brothers was convinced that the Vitaphone could be perfected and therefore promoted. The studio's release in 1926 of the silent film *Don Juan*, which boasted a synchronized musical score, successfully demonstrated the Vitaphone's capability, but it was Warner Brothers' release the following year of *The Jazz Singer*, with music plus dialogue (mainly in one scene), that would be the silent film industry's undoing.

Robert E. Sherwood, "The Silent Drama: *The Jazz Singer*," *Life*, vol. 90, October 27, 1927, p. 24.

In the following article, excerpted from a 1928 issue of *Life* magazine, film critic Robert E. Sherwood immediately understood the significance of *The Jazz Singer* as the harbinger of change in the silent film industry. Although the Vitaphone only provided a brief spurt of dialogue and song during the movie, quickly reverting back to subtitles and pantomime so typical of silent screen, it was clear to Sherwood that the Vitaphone would remain a fixture in the moving picture industry and that the magazine's silent film department had best seek a new title. The Vitaphone had justified its credibility, and despite Al Jolson's inability to act, his charisma as a singer had won audiences over: Warner Brothers had picked the perfect star.

Journalist Robert E. Sherwood was a film critic and motion picture editor for *Life* magazine from 1920 to 1928, but he is best known as the playwright who wrote *The Petrified Forest* and *Abe Lincoln in Illinois*, among others. He also was a distinguished screenwriter and wrote the Academy Award–winning film *The Best Years of Our Lives* (1946). He is also the author of a book on President Franklin D. Roosevelt.

There is one moment in "The Jazz Singer" that is fraught with tremendous significance.

Al Jolson, appearing as a Jewish youth, returns to his old home after years of wandering around the Pantages circuit. His strictly orthodox father has disowned him because he chose to sing mammy songs in music halls rather than chants in the synagogue; his mother, however, welcomes the prodigal with open arms.

Al sits down at the piano and sings "Blue Sky" for his mother. Thanks to the Vitaphone attachment, his marvelous voice rings out from the screen, the sound agreeing perfectly with the movements of his mobile lips, the wriggling of his shoulders, the nervous tapping of his feet.

After the song, there is a brief bit of spoken dialogue and then Al bursts into "Blue Sky" again. When he is half-way through the chorus, his father enters the room, realizes that his house is being profaned with jazz, and shouts, "Stop!"

At this point, the Vitaphone withdraws and "The Jazz Singer" returns to a routine of pantomime punctuated with sub-titles.

Such is the moment referred to in paragraph one—and when

it came, I for one suddenly realized that the end of the silent drama is in sight, that I shall have to find a new name for this department, and that several attractive heading designs by John Held, Jr., will have to be thrown out.

Al Jolson and the Vitaphone Convince Audiences

There is no question of doubt that the Vitaphone justifies itself in "The Jazz Singer." Furthermore, it proves that talking movies are considerably more than a lively possibility: they are close to an accomplished fact.

"The Jazz Singer" isn't much of a moving picture, as moving pictures go. It has a good idea (taken from Samuel Raphaelson's play), but it has been hoked and sugared to a regrettable extent; and Al Jolson as an actor on the screen is only fair.

But when Al Jolson starts to sing . . . well, bring on your super-spectacles, your million-dollar thrills, your long-shots of Calvary against a setting sun, your close-ups of a glycerine tear on [actress] Norma Talmadge's cheek—I'll trade them all for one instant of any ham song that Al cares to put over, and the hammer it is, the better I'll like it.

The Future of Silent-Screen Stars

In view of the imminence of talking movies, I wonder what [actress] Clara Bow's voice will sound like. And I wonder whether the speeches that the Hollywood sub-title writers compose will be as painful to hear as they are to read.

Perhaps the silent drama had better remain silent until Miss Bow and the other stars have taken a few lessons in vocal culture, and until all the present sub-titlers have died or something.

EVENT 6 The Stock Market Crash Leads to a Global Economic Depression: October 1929

The Stock Market Crash and the Downward Economic Spiral

by Denis W. Brogan

On October 24, 1929, "Black Thursday," the U.S. stock market plummeted to an all-time record low, sending stock owners into a frenzied sell-off of 13 million shares. But by the end of day, after financial leaders found a means to stabilize the market, the worst appeared over. No one knew at the time that they had just witnessed the onset of the Great Depression, or, as author Denis W. Brogan calls it in the following article, "the greatest debacle known in the financial history of the United States and the world."

According to Brogan, the wakeup call for the crash was really in 1927 with the loosening of credit and in 1928 with the recession. This, coupled with the fact that many investors remained optimistic and confident during the initial stages of the crash, further paved the way to economic disaster.

Denis W. Brogan was a political scientist, historian, educator, and author. He lectured in American history at the University of London and in American government at the London School of Economics and Political Science.

It is seldom possible to identify a single day as the beginning of a new era or cycle, but a date on which the period of the New Deal [President Franklin D. Roosevelt's program of relief for Americans during the Great Depression, 1932] was born may plausibly be fixed. On October 24, 1929, as panic gripped the New York Stock Exchange, nearly thirteen million shares were sold in the greatest debacle known in the financial history of the United States and the world.

Warning Signs

Bitter hindsight was later to make it difficult for many to remember with what blind confidence they had supported the great bull market. Yet ever since the Federal Reserve Board had acted in the summer of 1927 to loosen credit, some critics had expressed apprehension and some men had prophesied distress if not disaster. In the spring of 1928 a sharp recession had shaken out many weak speculators, and suggested to prudent men that the time had come to pocket their profits; but these prudent folk were to be confounded by the experience of 1929, when prices soared higher than ever. They went up and up until they reached their peak on September 19. As they did so, the great majority listened to the "experts" who talked of a new day in American if not world economics.

The attempt of the Federal Reserve Board in 1929 to slow down the bull market had deserved a better response. Just before [Herbert] Hoover became President, it had warned member banks and the public that the Federal Reserve Act did not "contemplate the use of the resources of the Federal Reserve Banks for the creation or extension of speculative credit." But the weakness of mere exhortation was soon manifest. The National City Bank boldly defied the heads of the banking system. So did some great corporations like Bethlehem Steel. The boom market was not to be starved into sobriety; particularly when the profits of feeding it were so attractive, with new call money being lent [by brokers] on the eve of the crash at nearly 10 per cent [loans payable at the discretion of borrowers or on demand by lender]. Yet the Federal Reserve Board was right in showing uneasiness. Factory production began to decline in July; the peak of employment came in July and it began to fall early in October; building had been increasingly stagnant since 1925. Prudent European speculators were beginning to take alarm, and before the fatal day there had been several sharp breaks in stock prices. Indeed, though few suspected it, the great boom had reached its peak six weeks before the avalanche swept down on the market.

A Bold Stroke to Halt the Collapse Fails

When the catastrophic nature of the collapse became apparent on October 24 [often referred to as Black Thursday], the leaders of the New York financial world took hasty council. Panic had to be halted before it became uncontrollable; so the rulers of the market argued, and on that premise they acted. Morgan, National City, Chase, Guaranty Trust and Bankers Trust put up $240,000,000 and the chief Morgan broker [Richard Whitney] was sent in to buy [stock]. The very sight of Richard Whitney, the knowledge of what forces were behind him, stopped the rout. . . .

By the weekend the worst seemed to be over. But it was not, for on Monday the retreat was again a rout, and it was obvious that a crisis was developing which would test the American economy. [By Tuesday, October 29, the real crash, the market bottom fell completely, although there was a brief recovery in November that lasted four and a half months.]

Millions of Americans Are Affected

One of the distinguishing features of the stock-market crash of 1929 was the degree to which it involved millions of Americans who, a generation before, would have had no more direct concern with the latest speculative prices of stocks than with the latest prices of old masters. But the great bond sales of the First World War and the subsequent rumors of easy profits made by investment bred a new attitude toward the fascinating game of playing the market.

Money was sucked into the New York market by all the devices of high-powered salesmanship. It was money, at first, to float great industrial corporations like the Nash automobile company, to develop Cuba, and to fund the debts of Peru; it was money to reequip Germany. Then it was simply money for any promising speculation. By the spring of 1929, gambling had become respectable. Banks and brokers catering to it flourished like faro men in a gold rush. In the single year 1929, no less than $11,000,000,000 of new securities were marketed. Every great city had its jammed, overworked stock exchange, and many secondary cities boasted them too. At least one minor city of Pennsylvania was planning its own exchange as the crash came; it seemed as much a necessity for a rising community as a country club or a chamber of commerce. . . .

To be sure, there had been warning voices telling Main Street of the doubtful character of the benefits offered by Wall Street. But men knew that there were great speculators in the market and that prices were made and unmade by their decisions. . . .

The public was admonished in October, 1929, by the New York *World*, not to think that 1920 had come again. There was no post-war inflation to liquidate; there was comparative stability in the world markets; there was peace. Above all, there was the incomparable American productive machine. The great plants still stood, their slight slowing up in production disregarded. The fertile lands that had been so lavishly mortgaged were as fertile as ever. The great office buildings and apartment houses of so many cities from New York to Beaumont, Texas, still stood. Still greater towers were being thrust into the sky. The American people with its ingenuity, industry, and resources was unchanged. True, vast paper losses had been incurred. When a new bottom was reached in late November, the investors were thirty billion dollars poorer. But optimists held that it was only a paper loss. Prudent men like the elder and younger Rockefeller were buying good common stocks. Surely President Hoover was right when he said that the worst would be over in sixty days; surely Secretary [of the Treasury Andrew] Mellon was correct when he seemed to welcome the liquidation of merely speculative elements in the American economy. When Christmas came, the stores were as busy as ever, the worst seemed over, and it was reasonable to expect that in 1930 the short pull upwards would begin again.

Yet for hundreds of thousands the prospect remained grim enough. The fairy gold of easy profits had been counted on, and hostages had been given to fortune. Houses had been bought (on credit); cars had been bought (on credit); jewels had been bought (on credit); sons and daughters had been sent to college (on credit). The very speculations that had turned out so badly had been largely conducted on credit. At the height of the speculative craze it was estimated that 300,000,000 shares were being held on margin [on borrowed money from brokers], and sometimes the investor's contribution was only 10 per cent. Unable to put up adequate collateral, such men lost their investment. . . .

For those whose index of national health was the stock market, there seemed evidence in the early spring of 1930 that confidence in the power of the American economic machine was justified. Market prices did recover; there was even a little boom. The rulers of the nation and the market acted on the theory that all that was now seriously needed was a full restoration of confidence. The old Puritan comforts were argued: adversity was bracing; the nation and individuals alike would gain by the sharp lesson administered. For the greater part of the American population, such admonitions made sense. It was at worst a case of Paradise Mislaid, not Paradise Lost.

Facing the Hard Facts

This optimistic view overlooked the hard fact that even at the height of the boom there had been black patches on the golden quilt of national prosperity. In worked-out cotton lands of the South like Greene County in Georgia, poverty and economic despair were not new. In debt-encumbered rural areas in the Dakotas, there had been no great margin since the collapse of the war boom in 1920. In the declining textile towns of New England men and women had been despondent for years before 1929. The peak of the boom had been reached as far as manual workers were concerned some time before the stock market boiled over. There were probably at least two million unemployed even in the best months of 1929. And it was suspected that millions more were beginning to put unusual pressure on public and private charity.

When summer came on, it was evident that either confidence had not returned or that confidence was not enough. And even though the President's appeal to industry not to cut wages was heeded by many great corporations, it was ignored by others, and in any case was poor comfort for the mounting army of the unemployed. By autumn, faith in the industrial and political rulers of America was ebbing fast. . . .

Affairs did not take a turn for the better, and early in the new year, 1931, the man who had personified the endless golden day, ex-President Coolidge, announced flatly in his daily column: "This country is not in good condition." The statement was now a bitter truism. With the acceptance of that truism, there came into the American mind a growing sense of anger and disillusionment. . . . The tactics of preaching confidence [by President Hoover] now recoiled upon the heads of the preachers. The Republican promises of 1928 were recalled with irony, and an optimistic statement upon the speedy abolition of poverty once made by Mr. Hoover became a bitter byword.

Radical Groups Gain Followings

To the small zealous group of the American Communists, the depression seemed a vindication of their preaching. In vain they had talked about the inherent contradictions of capitalism in the golden day. Now they could point with ironical scorn at the men who had talked of an "economic revolution" which was to abolish class distinctions in a free competitive system. Among the educated classes, and especially the young professional writers, teachers, and technicians, they won some recruits. So did other radical groups. For a moment, the panacea of technocracy seemed the answer to tens of thousands perplexed by the sight of so much technical capacity and material resources unused. The inventor of this doctrine was an enemy of the money system. National accounts should be kept in units of energy, and with the free release of the national resources that would follow from throwing off thraldom to finance, every American family could have the equivalent of an annual income of $20,000. In their despair, thousands clutched at the hopes thus held out, and for months, technocracy was the main conventional theme of conversation. Its popularity was probably significant less of faith in the new doctrine than of doubt in the old order.

Poverty, Unemployment, and Despair

The condition of the masses meanwhile went from bad to desperate. Though nobody could do more than guess at the figures of the unemployed, certainly by the end of 1931 they numbered over ten million. Those who had work were often paid miserable wages. Wages in the Pittsburgh steel industry fell from $30 a week in 1929 to $15 in 1932; a worker in a Southern mill who complained that he got only $2 a day was told by an unemployed friend that he would take the job for a dollar a day. Servants were found to be working for their mere keep; shopgirls in New York were hired for $3 a week. In the boom days it could be complacently assumed that, apart from children and the physically handicapped, only the shiftless needed help, save in sudden emergencies of accidents, illness, or the loss of the breadwinner. For dealing with such cases there was an elaborate machinery of organized charity. Akron [Ohio], for example, had the Family Service Society, which in August, 1929, dealt with 257 cases. What was Akron to do when 5,000 cases a month appeared in 1932? . . .

By the summer of 1931, nobody could pretend that the unemployed were idle good-for-nothings who preferred not to work. They were everywhere, standing idle in the streets of stricken industrial towns, where one observer saw men "on the sidewalks clapping their hands in a queer way, obviously just to be doing something." The symbolic unemployed man of the depression was the apple seller who bought fruit cheap from worried producers and offered it to the more prosperous, who had, in these outstretched hands, a perpetual reminder of the national sickness.

Clergy and social workers reported with increasing distress on the effects of the depression upon home life. The father of the family, proud to be "a good provider," was now often the dependent of his children and his wife. Some families were strengthened by the ordeal; more were weakened. Tens of thousands of boys and thousands of girls took to the roads. Soon the "hobo jungles" were full of youthful recruits, and the railroad police gave up attempting to keep them from stealing rides. Whole families moved on in a vague search for a better place to live or merely because they had no place to live at all. They begged for handouts; they stole and parched corn. Men lost skill and lost hope.

Bank Failures

While it was mainly on the poor that the greatest suffering fell, tens of thousands of once prosperous people were precipitated to the bottom of the economic scale, beyond all hope of recovery. New disasters added to the general misery. The failure of the Bank of United States in New York swept away the savings of multitudes of immigrants who, deceived by the name, felt that the Federal Government or some other official body should make good their losses. The collapse of the Swedish match empire of Kreuger and Toll ruined thousands of a more prosperous and theoretically more prudent class from Boston to Seattle. All over America, banks closed by the hundreds until few of the great cities did not have a record of the sudden suspension or the long and futile struggle of some prominent financial establishment.

The Government's Role

Bank failures became so great a threat, indeed, that the Administration was forced to depart from its trust in the curative forces of a free economy. After an ineffective attempt to get the strong banks to support the weak, it set up the Reconstruction Finance Corporation [RFC] (January, 1932) with Federal funds to support threatened banks, railroads, states, and cities. The social strain of further liquidation might have brought about the collapse of the whole debt structure, for debt was one of the great problems of the crisis. While the national income fell to less than half what it had been in 1929, the burden of debt was little altered. The holders of titles to money were the last sufferers. Indeed, dividends hardly dropped at all in the first two years of the depression. The contrast between the losses of the sellers of money and the sellers of labor was striking. . . .

Against this background of differential suffering, it was hard to take calmly the refusal of the Federal Government to help alleviate such widespread misery. True, the Reconstruction Finance Corporation was authorized to lend money to states and other governmental units for relief work, but President Hoover stood firmly by the doctrine of local responsibility for relief, regardless of the insolvency of many cities and counties, of the reluctance of bankers to lend, and the frequent constitutional impotence of local governments to borrow. When it was revealed that the head of a great bank had managed to avoid taxes on an immense income by creating fictitious losses, and that much of the income of the richer classes was in tax-free bonds; when a Senate committee began to expose the rigging of the markets, the creation of pools, and the sale of next to worthless bonds, the patience of the people with financial orthodoxy declined. A revolt against Congressional leaders of both parties prevented a general Federal sales tax, and in each year after 1930, the Federal deficit grew to what then seemed astronomically dangerous heights.

The Homeless Abound

Despite the RFC, banks continued to fail and railroads to pass into the hands of receivers. The real estate market was also demoralized. Its ailments had been one of the causes of the depression, and the failure of the investment house of S.W. Strauss and Company was as symbolic a disaster as the closing of the Bank of United States. Socially more important was the long history of evictions. Rents were often unpayable, and all over the country hundreds of thousands of tenants were turned out while hundreds of thousands of owners lost their mortgaged homes.

Communists were quick to support resistance and to move tenants and furniture back as fast as they were moved out. But such tactics were no more of an answer than the old spiritual sung by threatened Chicago Negroes: "I shall not, I shall not be moved." They were moved. Others abandoned expensive apartments and unpaid-for furniture and took what shelter they could find. In New York, a reporter found a husband and wife living in a cave in Central Park. Some slept in home-made sheds. Some lived with their families; in many cases they went back to the family farm. But the farmers were often threatened with eviction. Millions of acres were forfeited.

Local Governments Suffer

The threatened bankruptcy of local government was one ingredient of the bitter draught. Some cities could not afford an adequate police force. Every luxury of government was ruthlessly pruned. Libraries bought no books; hospitals got along with inadequate staffs and supplies; and even the pride of American democracy, the school system, sometimes seemed threatened with destruction. Teachers' pay was cut and cut again. Schools were opened late, were badly heated and badly cleaned. In some areas they did not open at all. . . .

A Brief Window of Hope

But while [President Hoover] waited for the curative power of nature to work, luck was against him. For a brief moment in the summer of 1931, a bold stroke by the President was seen as a turning point. He induced Congressional leaders to agree to a year's suspension of the European war debts in return for a suspension of the reparations due from Germany. It was becoming an Administration theory that the sickness of Europe was preventing the convalescence of the United States. . . . But the debt moratorium of 1931 had no permanent effects. England went off the gold standard, world trade still shrank, and the economic plight of the United States grew steadily worse.

The revolt of the farmers was accompanied by a rising demand of veterans for a war bonus. Congress did something for them. It allowed (over the President's veto) the advancing of 50 per cent of the value of the "adjusted service certificates" of the veterans, a step which led to the underwriting in 1931 of one and a quarter billion dollars' worth of veterans' borrowings. It was unorthodox but it did enable a section of the American people to pay its debts; and that was not unimportant. In 1932 it was estimated that "uncollectible retail debts" amounted to $600,000,000, three times the average of 1929.

The Spiral Continues

Nature seemed to conspire to perplex the leaders of the nation. At a time when oil prices were ruinously low, great oil discoveries in eastern Texas threatened to ruin the already harassed producers in older fields. Cotton dropped from 16 cents a pound in 1929 to 5.4 cents a pound in 1932. Wheat fell from $1.00 a bushel to 31.6 cents. The index of industrial production declined from 119 in 1929 to 64 in 1932. National income went down by more than half, and national wealth by more than a quarter. The growing paralysis was reflected in small things and in big. In Akron, building permits and dog licenses alike declined from 1930 to 1931 by two-thirds. There seemed to be no end to the spiral of decline.

E V E N T **6** **The Stock Market Crash Leads to a Global Economic Depression: October 1929**

The Crash Ignites an Economic Collapse Worldwide

by Lewis Browne

There seemed no end to the Wall Street nightmare, according to author Lewis Browne. The sudden fluctuations in an otherwise booming market throughout September 1929 that caused alarm, and were then dismissed as "technical adjustments," proved disastrous on October 29, when the market suddenly bottomed out and crashed. In the following article Browne recaps the downward slide that led to that eventful day, including the criminal deception by trusted financial experts who apparently encouraged typical investors to buy again. Although many applauded the sudden miracle and followed this advice, the so-called trusted experts quietly withdrew their money in lieu of bankruptcy

Meanwhile, President Herbert Hoover gave a rather ineffective speech that was meant to encourage but, as Browne points out, was "shakily asserted." For those Americans who read in the paper of the horrendous losses by investors in the crash, but knew nothing of the stock market, the numbers likely meant little. Yet the effects of those losses would ultimately involve them as well, causing undue suffering in a dark period of U.S. history that Browne asserts was a time of "evil days and months and years." What became known as

Lewis Browne, *Something Went Wrong: A Summation of Modern History*. New York: The Macmillan Company, 1942.

the Great Depression would begin to spread across the United States in 1930 and eventually spread to other nations.

Lewis Browne once said, "I doubt whether I can possibly live long enough to write all the books for which I already have titles." As a historian and biographer with a flair for drama, his passion for writing resulted in a number of books ranging from Jewish and Christian history to modern history.

Then came the Deluge. Thunder pealed all through September 1929, but the great wise men on Wall Street—and even more the little wise guys on Main Street—refused to take heed. The sudden and recurrent breaks in the stock market were dismissed as "technical adjustments." There were further and sharper breaks in early October; but still the speculators remained bullish. One of the high priests at the National Shrine, Mr. Charles E. Mitchell of the National City Bank, looked up from his altar and pontificated: "The American Markets generally are now in a healthy condition."

Deception Before the Fall

Instantly prices rallied—but only to sag again the next week. On October 23 there was a break that carried some stocks down more than ninety points. Knees began to quake then, and faces grayed. The next morning a number of stocks could find no buyers at any price, and then even the high priests became alarmed. They had advanced more than six and a half billion dollars to the speculators. Should they call in those loans and start a panic? Or should they sit tight and risk bankruptcy? A conference was hastily summoned in the Holy of Holies—the directors' room of J.P. Morgan & Company—and throughout the land anxious hearts pounded louder than the tickers. Finally, at 1:15 P.M., word came of the decision. Mr. Richard Whitney, then floor-operator for the Morgan company—later floor-sweeper in Sing Sing [prison]—strode into the Exchange and bid for a block of U.S. Steel at twelve points above the current price. Salvation! Immediately stocks ceased to fall. Some even began to climb.

Not for long, however. The public, reassured by the miracle on Black Thursday, started to buy again. But those who had worked the miracle began to sell. Quietly, gently, they eased themselves of their burdens. Four days this continued, four fevered days during which all who were supposed to be in the know talked "long," and all who were behind the show sold "short."

Then, on October 29, it happened.

The storm finally broke, and it tore the bottom right out from under the market. The rush of selling orders jammed the tickers, choked the telephone wires, wrecked the teletype machines. Within half an hour of the opening of the Exchange, more than a million shares had been dumped on the counters. By noon the volume of trading had passed the eight million mark. When the closing gong tolled the end of that stark raving day, nearly sixteen and a half million shares had changed hands. The National Shrine had become the Wailing Wall.

Assessing the Damage

The Big Bull Market had collapsed. The vaunted New Era was no more. What had happened so often before, had happened once again: having begun by losing their heads, the businessmen had ended by losing their shirts. And even their hides, this time. The Panic of 1837 had been bad, that of 1857 even worse, and in 1875 and 1893 others had come which had proved still worse. Yet all those four together did not equal the one that now befell the United States. The investment structure became a shambles. What had so long been called "securities," became mere paper flying before the wind.

At first all authoritative voices insisted on screaming that there was no cause for alarm. "Don't sell America short!" they screamed. The President naturally refrained from screaming; he spoke calmly, as became one in so august an office. But what Mr. Hoover said calmly might just as well have been screamed, for it was no less delusory, and no more effective. Time and again he cleared his throat, moistened his lips, and shakily asserted: "We have now passed the worst. . . . Prosperity is just around the corner." But where was the corner?

Conditions Worsen

The panic deepened and spread. During 1931 alone some 2000 banks had to close their doors; 28,000 business firms went bankrupt. That same year 39% of the largest corporations in the country lost money, and half of the major railroads went into receivership.

And conditions grew even worse in 1932.

People ceased to call it merely a panic; it had become The Depression. A corner had been reached at last, but behind it lurked prostration. Goods would not move. No matter at what price they were offered, they would not move.

By January 1931, wheat was selling at the lowest price in two hundred and fifty years. Nevertheless, millions of poor people failed to eat more bread. By the end of that year the wholesale price of textiles was down 32%. Nevertheless those millions failed to buy new clothes. It was not that they did not want such things. They wanted them so badly that they were ready to steal them. But they could not buy them. They had always lacked cash, and now the merchants would not give them credit. How could one give credit to people who had no jobs?

For unemployment had increased appallingly. Even before October 1929, there were already some 2,000,000 jobless people in the country. A year later there were 4,000,000; two years later, 7,000,000; three years later, 13,000,000. The national economy went into a tailspin. More unemployment meant less purchasing power, and therefore still less manufacturing, and therefore still more unemployment, and therefore . . . By the end of 1932 there were 35% fewer people at work in the factories than in 1929. To make matters worse, those who did have jobs were getting lower wages. Factory payrolls had fallen off by 54%. To make matters still worse, agricultural income, which had been low even during the Boom, sank actually lower by some 57%. The net result was that common purchasing power was reduced by some thirty billion dollars—approximately as much as the country had spent to fight the World War.

That was why goods failed to move. The masses lacked the means to get at them. Millions had to spend all they could earn or beg merely to lay hold of enough food to keep flesh on their bones. If they had anything left over—often even if they hadn't—they helped themselves to liquor and tobacco. Of all the major industries, only liquor—despite that it was illegal—and tobacco seemed able to prosper.

Evil days fell on the land, evil days and months and years. Breadlines formed in the cities, and foul squatter settlements—"Hoovervilles," they were ironically called—gathered like scabs over the city dumps. Dispossessed farmers sold their plows and mules, piled their families into old Fords, and started wandering in search of a place where there was food. A horde of ex-soldiers marched on Washington and encamped there in shacks until driven off by fire and tear-gas. Skilled workers became hoboes; bookkeepers became hoboes; teachers, lawyers, even former bankers became hoboes. Boys just out of high school, and girls who dressed like boys, began to rove about in packs. Crime increased everywhere; gangsterism broke all bounds. Evil days fell on the land.

Conditions Were Even Worse Abroad

And it was even worse abroad. A good deal of the world had been living off American capital ever since the War. Eleven billion dollars had come pouring out of the United States between 1917 and 1924, and another three billion dollars between 1924 and 1928. Most of the money had gone to Europe, where it had been used first to set the economy back on its feet, and then to keep it moving. Once this support was withdrawn, only one thing could happen.

Europe's economy collapsed.

In a sense it was dragged down, for the Americans did not simply stop lending money to Europe; they began to demand that what had already been borrowed should be returned. They called in their short-term loans, and asked for the interest on the long-term ones. Moreover, they wanted payment in cash. They would not take goods. They already had more goods than they knew what to do with. They wanted gold.

For a while they got gold. But after a year the supply began to give out in Central Europe, and then the situation grew critical. By May 1931 the chief bank in Vienna began to totter, and its collapse threatened to drag the entire nation into bankruptcy. The German banks, being heavily involved in Austria's economy, rushed to the rescue. This, however, left them so weakened that they in turn began to cave in. The British banks struggled to shore them up, only to weaken themselves in further turn. All Europe teetered on the brink of financial chaos. The whole world teetered there.

Hoover Responds Too Late

At the last moment President Hoover took it upon himself to propose a year's moratorium on international debts. Too late. In July every bank in Germany had to close its doors. In September Great Britain had to refuse to honor its notes in gold. By the end of 1931 fourteen other nations—among them Sweden, Japan, Siam, Chile, Persia—were off the gold standard.

Half the world had gone over the brink.

The blame was laid, of course, at the door of the United States. Though this country had ceased to demand gold, it was still refusing to buy goods. Formerly it had been the world's largest customer for raw materials, and the second largest for manufactured wares. But now, with the domestic markets glutted, and the foreign ones choked, importation necessarily had to decline. By the end of 1931 the United States was importing less than a third as much as in 1928. That meant unemployment in the tin mines in Malaya, the silk mills in Japan, the rubber groves in Java, the coffee plantations in Brazil. It meant unemployment in the English woolen mills, the German dye works, the Czech glove factories, the Italian felt looms. By the summer of 1932 there were nearly 14,000,000 Europeans out of work. In Germany half the young men between the ages of 16 and 32 were without jobs.

The Horror Spreads

The horror spread from the cities to the villages. Once the urban masses began to pull in their belts, food began to fall in price. Debt-ridden farmers found that interest charges which they had once been able to meet with a hundred bushels of wheat could not be settled now with less than two hundred. That drove them still deeper into debt, forced them to sell their cattle, finally left them bare. The word *mortgage* began to recover its original meaning—"death-grip." Peasants in China had to let their sons become bandits. In Japan they hired out their daughters as whores. In the Balkans they took to wearing animal skins and eating rats.

Despair stalked the earth. Men could not understand this evil that had befallen them. Had it been a famine, they would at least have seen a reason for their hunger. Had there been an earthquake, they would have known why they were shelterless. But food was rotting in the granaries and fields; everywhere shops and dwellings stood empty. Yet millions throughout the world were begging for a crust to eat, millions were sleeping under bridges or in the open fields.

Something had gone wrong. Everybody knew now that something had gone very wrong.

EVENT 7 **Mahatma Gandhi's Salt March Strikes a Blow for Indian Independence: March 1930**

Gandhi's Salt March Empowers Indians

by Louis Fischer

In 1930, Indian leader Mahatma Gandhi (1869–1948) was about to lead his country in an act of civil disobedience that would further pave the way to India's independence. India had been a colony of England since 1858. Although England had formed a mutual government with India in 1919, allowing Indians to rule through the Indian National Congress, India's government was still under the watchful eye of local British officials and Parliament in London. Similarly, India's law enforcement consisted of a large native (Indian) police force commanded by a small group of British officers. This lack of self-rule plus a glaring lack of social reform, as in the status of the poor and India's caste the "untouchables," frustrated Gandhi and others, resulting in a nonviolent resistance movement in the 1920s against British injustice (e.g., low wages and high prices of goods) that convinced hundreds of thousands that freedom was possible.

But the movement was not without violence, and by 1930, radical leaders in Congress were demanding India's full independence by year's end—by force if necessary. A bloody showdown between Indians and British seemed likely. Strongly opposed to violence, Gandhi immediately sought a new form of nonviolent civil disobedience that would not only get England's attention, but would satisfy the radicals in Congress. The result would be an event that united most of India in the fight for independence. Following is an article excerpted from Louis Fischer's *The Life of Mahatma Gandhi*

Louis Fischer, *The Life of Mahatma Gandhi*. New York: Harper & Row, 1950.

(1950), describing Gandhi's famous Salt March to the sea and its long-range effects.

After a two-hundred-mile journey, Gandhi arrived at the Arabian Sea with a crowd of several thousand. There, garbed in his familiar peasant attire of spun cloth, Gandhi officially broke the British Salt Laws by drawing seawater to produce salt for sale. News of Gandhi's act, according to Fischer, spread like fire and before long, contraband salt was in abundance everywhere, providing a commodity that the British had controlled access to and taxed. The British monopoly on salt production and sale was clearly an injustice that had seeded resentment in all. The defiance spilled over into other acts of disobedience, according to Fischer, uniting the nation even further. In the end, the Salt March had given Indians a new national identity, but inwardly, it had given them the courage to fight against injustice and inequality. India would not achieve independence until 1947, but today Gandhi is still considered the father of India and is best remembered for his nonviolent principles in achieving political and social progress. He has also inspired civil rights leaders such as Martin Luther King Jr. and many others.

Louis Fischer won the American Historical Association Watumull Prize in 1951 for *The Life of Mahatma Gandhi*, a book later used in the making of a Hollywood film on Gandhi. His other writings include numerous historical books published between 1926 and 1973. Early in his career, he was a public school teacher, and later an overseas correspondent, known particularly for his firsthand knowledge of Soviet Russia.

Gandhi was a reformer of individuals, hence his concern for the means whereby India's liberation might be achieved. If the means corrupted the individual, the loss would be greater than the gain.

Gandhi knew that the re-education of a nation was a slow process, and he was not usually in a hurry unless prodded by events or by men reacting to those events. Left to himself, he would not have forced the issue of independence in 1930. But now the die was cast; [the Indian National] Congress had decreed a campaign for independence. The leader therefore became an obedient soldier.

During the weeks after the stirring New Year's Eve independence ceremony, Gandhi searched for a form of civil disobedience that left no opening for violence.

Gandhi's monumental abhorrence of violence stemmed from the Jainist and Buddhist infusions into his Hinduism but, particularly, from his love of human beings. Every reformer, crusader, and dictator avows his undying devotion to the anonymous mass; Gandhi had an apparently endless capacity to love the individual men, women, and children who crowded his life. . . .

Rabindranath Tagore [Indian poet], for whom Gandhi had the deepest veneration, was in the neighborhood of Sabarmati Ashram [Gandhi's community] and came for a visit on January 18th. He inquired what Gandhi had in store for the country in 1930. "I am furiously thinking night and day," Gandhi replied, "and I do not see any light coming out of the surrounding darkness."

The situation made Gandhi apprehensive. "There is a lot of violence in the air," he said. The British government had altered the exchange rate of the rupee so that India might import more from Lancashire [England]; the Indian middle class suffered. The [U.S.] Wall Street crash of October 1929, and the spreading world economic depression hit the Indian peasant. Working-class unrest was mounting for all these reasons and because of the government's persecution of labor organizers. Again, as in 1919 to 1921, a number of young Indians saw an opportunity of striking a bloody blow for freedom. [British massacre in 1919 changed Indian loyalty and spurred revolt.]

Civil disobedience in these circumstances involved "undoubted risks," but the only alternative was "armed rebellion." Gandhi's confidence remained unshaken.

For six weeks, Gandhi had been waiting to hear the "Inner Voice." This, as he interpreted it, had no Joan-of-Arc connotations. "The 'Inner Voice,'" he wrote, "may mean a message from God or from the Devil, for both are wrestling in the human breast. Acts determine the nature of the voice."

Gandhi Informs British Viceroy of Planned Civil Disobedience

Presently, Gandhi seemed to have heard the Voice. . . . On March 2, 1930, Gandhi sent a long letter to the [British] Viceroy serving notice that civil disobedience would begin in nine days.

It was the strangest communication the head of a government ever received:

Dear Friend, Before embarking on civil disobedience and taking the risk I have dreaded to take all these years, I would fain approach you and find a way out.

My personal faith is absolutely clear. I cannot intentionally hurt anything that lives, much less human beings, even though they may do the greatest wrong to me and mine. Whilst, therefore, I hold the British rule to be a curse, I do not intend harm to a single Englishman or to any legitimate interest he may have in India. . . .

And why do I regard the British rule as a curse?

It has impoverished the dumb millions by a system of progressive exploitation and by a ruinous expensive military and civil administration which the country can never afford.

It has reduced us politically to serfdom. It has sapped the foundations of our culture. And by the policy of cruel disarmament, it has degraded us spiritually. . . .

I fear . . . there never has been any intention of granting . . . Dominion Status [self-rule] to India in the immediate future. . . .

It seems as clear as daylight that responsible British statesmen do not contemplate any alteration in British policy that might adversely affect Britain's commerce with India. . . . If nothing is done to end the process of exploitation, India must be bled with an ever increasing speed. . . .

Let me put before you some of the salient points.

The terrific pressure of land revenue . . . must undergo considerable modification in an Independent India . . . the whole revenue system has to be so revised as to make the peasant's good its primary concern. But the British system seems to be designed to crush the very life out of him. Even the salt he must use to live is so taxed as to make the burden fall heaviest on him. . . . The tax shows itself still more burdensome on the poor man when it is remembered that salt is the one thing he must eat more than the rich man. . . . The drink and drug revenue, too, is derived from the poor. It saps the foundations both of their health and morals.

The iniquities sampled above are maintained in order to carry on a foreign administration, demonstrably the most expensive in the world. Take your own salary. It is over 21,000 rupees [about $7,000] per month, besides many other indirect additions. . . . You are getting over 700 rupees a day against India's average income of less than two annas [four cents] per day. Thus, you are getting much over five thousand times India's average income.

The British Prime Minister is getting only ninety times Britain's average income. On bended knee, I ask you to ponder over this phenomenon. . . .

What is true of the Viceregal salary is true generally of the whole administration. . . . Nothing but organized non-violence can check the organized violence of the British government. . . .

My ambition is no less than to convert the British people through non-violence, and thus make them see the wrong they have done to India. I do not seek to harm your people. I want to serve them even as I want to serve my own. . . .

If the [Indian] people join me, as I expect they will, the sufferings they will undergo, unless the British nation sooner retraces its steps, will be enough to melt the stoniest hearts.

The plan through civil disobedience will be to combat such evils as I have sampled out. . . . I respectfully invite you to pave the way for the immediate removal of those evils, and thus open a way for a real conference between equals. . . . But if you cannot see your way to deal with these evils, and if my letter makes no appeal to your heart, on the eleventh day of this month I shall proceed with such co-workers of the Ashram as I can take, to disregard the provisions of the Salt Laws [a crime to possess salt not bought from the British government]. . . .

This letter is not in any way intended as a threat but [it] is a simple and sacred duty peremptory on a civil resister. Therefore, I am having it specially delivered by a young English friend who believes in the Indian cause. . . .

I remain

Your sincere friend,

M.K. Gandhi. . . .

The Salt March to the Sea Begins

Irwin [the Viceroy] chose not to reply. His secretary sent a four-line acknowledgment saying, "His Excellency . . . regrets to learn that you contemplate a course of action which is clearly bound to involve violation of the law and danger to the public peace."

This law-and-order note, which disdained to deal with matters of justice and policy, caused Gandhi to say, "On bended knee I asked for bread and I received stone instead." Irwin refused to see Gandhi. Nor did he have him arrested. "The government," Gandhi declared, "is puzzled and perplexed." It was dangerous not to arrest the rebel, and dangerous to arrest him.

As March 11th neared, India bubbled with excitement and curiosity. Scores of foreign and domestic correspondents dogged Gandhi's footsteps in the ashram; what exactly would he do? Thousands surrounded the village and waited. The excitement spread abroad. Cables kept the Ahmedabad [near Gandhi's home] post office humming. "God guard you," the Reverend Dr. John Haynes Holmes [U.S. clergyman and reformer] wired from New York.

Gandhi felt it was the "opportunity of a lifetime."

On March 12th, prayers having been sung, Gandhi and seventy-eight male and female members of the ashram, whose identities were published in *Young India* [Gandhi's own newspaper] for the benefit of the police, left Sabarmati for Dandi, due south from Ahmedabad. Gandhi leaned on a lacquered bamboo staff one inch thick and 54 inches long with an iron tip. Following winding dirt roads from village to village, he and his seventy-eight disciples walked two hundred miles in twenty-four days. "We are marching in the name of God," Gandhi said.

Peasants sprinkled the roads and strewed leaves on them. Every settlement in the line of march was festooned and decorated with India's national colors. From miles around, peasants gathered to kneel by the roadside as the pilgrims passed. Several times a day, the marchers halted for a meeting where the Mahatma and others exhorted the people to wear khadi [handspun cotton] abjure alcohol and drugs, abandon child marriage, keep clean, live purely, and—when the signal came—break the Salt Laws.

He had no trouble walking. "Less than twelve miles a day in two stages with not much luggage," he said. "Child's play!" Several became fatigued and footsore, and had to ride in a bullock cart. A horse was available for Gandhi throughout the march but he never used it. "The modern generation is delicate, weak, and much pampered," Gandhi commented. He was sixty-one. He spun [cloth] every day for an hour and kept a diary and required each ashramite [from his ashram] to do likewise.

In the area traversed, over three hundred village headmen gave up their government jobs. The inhabitants of a village would accompany Gandhi to the next village. Young men and women attached themselves to the marching column; when Gandhi reached the sea at Dandi on April 5th, his small ashram band had grown into a non-violent army several thousand strong.

The entire night of April 5th, the ashramites prayed, and early in the morning they accompanied Gandhi to the sea. He dipped into the water, returned to the beach, and there picked up some salt left by the waves. Mrs. Sarojini Naidu [famous Indian poet], standing by his side, cried, "Hail, Deliverer." Gandhi had broken the British law, which made it a punishable crime to possess salt not obtained from the British government salt monopoly. Gandhi, who had not used salt for six years, called it a "nefarious monopoly." Salt, he said, is as essential as air and water, and in India all the more essential to the hard-working, perspiring poor man and his beasts because of the tropical heat.

Had Gandhi gone by train or automobile to make salt, the effect would have been considerable. But to walk for twenty-four days and rivet the attention of all India, to trek across a countryside saying, "Watch, I am about to give a signal to the nation," and then to pick up a pinch of salt in publicized defiance of the mighty government and thus become a criminal, that required imagination, dignity, and the sense of showmanship of a great artist. It appealed to the illiterate peasant, and it appealed to a sophisticated critic and sometime fierce opponent of Gandhi's like Subhas Chandra Bose, who compared the Salt March to "Napoleon's march to Paris on his return from Elba." [Bose belonged to the Indian National Congress but opposed Gandhi's nonviolence policy.]

The act performed, Gandhi withdrew from the scene. India had its cue. Gandhi had communicated with it by lifting up some grains of salt.

Civil Disobedience Spreads and the Police React

The next act was an insurrection without arms. Every villager on India's long seacoast went to the beach or waded into the sea with a pan to make salt. The police began mass arrests. Ramdas, third son of Gandhi, with a large group of ashramites, was arrested. Pandit Malaviya [active Congress member] and other moderate co-operators resigned from the [Indian] Legislative Assembly [a body that makes laws in cooperation with the British]. The police began to use violence. Civil resisters never resisted arrest; but they resisted the confiscation of the salt they had made, and Mahadev Desai [Gandhi's secretary] reported cases where such Indians were beaten and bitten in the fingers by constables. Congress' volunteers openly sold contraband salt in cities. Many were arrested and sentenced to short prison terms. In Delhi, a meeting of fifteen thousand persons heard Pandit Malaviya appeal to the audience to boycott foreign cloth; he himself bought some illegal salt after his speech. The police raided the Congress party headquarters in Bombay where salt was being made in pans on the roof. A crowd of sixty thousand assembled. Hundreds were handcuffed or their arms fastened with ropes and led off to jail. In Ahmedabad, ten thousand people obtained illegal salt from Congress in the first week after the act at Dandi. They paid what they could; if they had no money they got it free. The salt lifted by Gandhi from the beach was sold to a Dr. Kanuga, the highest bidder, for 1,600 rupees. Jawaharlal Nehru, the president of Congress, was arrested in Allahabad under the Salt Acts and sentenced to six months' imprisonment. The agitation and disobedience spread to the turbulent regions of the Maharashtra and Bengal. In Calcutta, the Mayor, J.M. Sengupta, read seditious literature aloud at a public meeting and urged non-wearing of foreign textiles. He was put in prison for six months. Picketing of liquor shops and foreign cloth shops commenced throughout India. Girls and ladies from aristocratic families and from families where purdah [child marriage] had been observed came out into the streets to demonstrate. Police became vindictive and kicked resisters in sensitive parts. Civil resistance began in the province of Bihar. Seventeen Bihar Satyagrahis ["truth warriors"; of the same movement Gandhi belonged to] including resigned members of [Indian] Legislative Councils, were sentenced to periods of . . . six months to two years in prison. A Swami who had lived in South Africa received two and a half years. Teachers, professors, and students made salt at the sea and inland and were marched to jails in batches. Kishorlal Mashruwala, a faithful disciple of Gandhi, and Jamnalal Bajaj, a rich friend of Gandhi's, were sentenced to two years' incarceration. In Karachi, the police fired on a demonstration; two young volunteers were killed. "Bihar has been denuded of almost all its leaders," Mahadev Desai wrote, "but the result has been the opening of many more salt centers." Congress distributed literature explaining simple methods of producing salt. . . . Leaders of the national Congress were arrested in Bombay. Devadas Gandhi [son of Gandhi] was sentenced to three months' imprisonment in Delhi. The salt movement and the arrests and imprisonments spread to Madras, the Punjab, and the Carnatic (Karnatak). Many towns observed hartals [strikes] when Congress leaders were arrested. At Patna, in Bihar, a huge mass of thousands moved out of the city to march to a spot where salt could be made. The police blocked the highway. The crowd stayed and slept on the road and in the fields for forty hours. Rajendra Prasad [future first president of India], who was present and told the story, received orders from the police officer to disperse the crowd. He refused. The officer announced that he would charge with cavalry. The crowd did not move. As the horses galloped forward, the men and women threw themselves flat on the ground. The horses stopped and did not trample them. Constables then proceeded to lift the demonstrators and place them in trucks for transportation to prison. Other demonstrators replaced them. Mahadev Desai was arrested for bringing in a load of salt. In villages, millions of peasants were preparing their own salt. The British pressed local officials to cope with the problem. The officials resigned. . . . The speaker of the Legislative Assembly, resigned. A large group of prominent women appealed to Lord Irwin [the Viceroy] to prohibit the sale of intoxicating beverages. At Karachi, fifty thousand people watched as salt was made on the seashore. The crowd was so dense the policemen were surrounded and could make no arrests. At Peshawar, the key to the volatile northwest Frontier Province, an armored car, in which the Deputy Police Commissioner was seated, first ran full-tilt into a crowd and then machine-gunned it, killing seventy and wounding about one hundred. In parts of Bengal, in the United Provinces, and in Gujarat, peasants refused to pay rent and the land tax. The government tried to place all nationalist newspapers under censorship, whereupon most of them voluntarily suspended publication. Congress provincial offices were sealed and their property and office paraphernalia confiscated. Rajagopalachari [future first Indian governor general] was arrested in Madras and given a nine months' sentence. The wild Afridi tribe, in the northwest frontier Tribal Area, attacked British patrols. In the city of Chittagong, Bengal, a band of violent revolutionists raided the arsenal to seize arms. Some were killed.

Gandhi Arrested

The Viceroy, says Irwin's biographer, "had filled the jails with no less than sixty thousand political offenders." Estimates ran as high as a hundred thousand. "A mere recital of the action taken by him during this time," the biography affirms, "belies once for all the legend that he was a weak Viceroy. Those who were responsible for executing his orders testify that his religious convictions seemed to reinforce the very ruthlessness of his policy of suppression. . . ."

A month after Gandhi touched salt at the Dandi beach, India was seething in angry revolt. But, except at Chittagong, there was no Indian violence, and nowhere was there any Congress violence. Chauri Chaura in 1922 had taught India a lesson [residents attacked a police station]. Because they treasured the movement Gandhi had conjured into being, and lest he cancel it, they abstained from force.

May 4th, Gandhi's camp was at Karadi, a village near Dandi. He had gone to sleep on a cot under a shed beneath the branches of an old mango tree. Several disciples slept by his side. Elsewhere in the grove, other ashramites were in deep slumber. At 12:45 A.M., in the night of May 4th to 5th, heavy steps were heard. Thirty Indian policemen armed with rifles, pistols, and lances, two Indian officers, and the British District Magistrate of Surat invaded the leafy compound. A party of armed constables entered Gandhi's shed and the English officer turned the flashlight on Gandhi's face. Gandhi awoke, looked about him, and said to the Magistrate, "Do you want me?"

"Are you Mohandas Karamchand Gandhi?" the Magistrate asked for the sake of form.

Gandhi admitted it.

The officer said he had come to arrest him.

"Please give me time for my ablutions," Gandhi said politely.

The Magistrate agreed. . . .

Gandhi loved it in jail. "I have been quite happy and making up for arrears in sleep," he wrote Miss Madeline Slade [Gandhi's British disciple and coworker] a week after his imprisonment. He was treated extremely well; the prison goat was milked in his presence. . . .

Followers Continue the Revolt at Dharasana Salt Works

Just before his arrest, Gandhi had drafted a letter to the Viceroy announcing his intention, "God willing," to raid the Dharasana Salt Works with some companions. God, apparently, was not willing, but the companions proceeded to effect the plan. Mrs. Sarojini Naidu, the poet, led twenty-five hundred volunteers to the site 150 miles north of Bombay and, after morning prayers, warned them that they would be beaten "but," she said, "you must not resist; you must not even raise a hand to ward off a blow."

Webb Miller, the well-known correspondent of the United Press who died in England during the Second World War, was on the scene and described the proceedings. Manilal Gandhi [son of Gandhi] moved forward at the head of the marchers and approached the great salt pans, which were surrounded by ditches and barbed wire and guarded by four hundred Surat policemen under the command of six British officers. "In complete silence, the Gandhi men drew up and halted a hundred yards from the stockade. A picked column advanced from the crowd, waded the ditches, and approached the barbed-wire stockade." The police officers ordered them to retreat. They continued to advance. "Suddenly," Webb Miller reported, "at a word of command, scores of native policemen rushed upon the advancing marchers and rained blows on their heads with their steel-shod lathis. Not one of the marchers even raised an arm to fend off the blows. They went down like ten-pins. . . . "Although everyone knew," Webb Miller wrote, "that within a few minutes he would be beaten down, perhaps killed, I could detect no signs of wavering or fear. They marched steadily, with heads up, without the encouragement of music or cheering or any possibility that they might escape serious injury or death. The police rushed out and methodically and mechanically beat down the second column. There was no fight, no struggle; the marchers simply walked forward till struck down.". . .

Hour after hour stretcher-bearers carried back a stream of inert, bleeding bodies."

A British officer approached Mrs. Naidu, touched her arm, and said, "Sarojini Naidu, you are under arrest." She shook off his hand. "I'll come," she declared, "but don't touch me." Manilal was also arrested.

"By eleven [in the morning]," Webb Miller continued, "the heat had reached 116 and the activities of the Gandhi volunteers subsided." He went to the temporary hospital and counted 320 injured, many of them still unconscious, others in agony from the body and head blows. Two men had died. The same scenes were repeated for several days.

A New India Emerges

India was now free. Technically, legally, nothing had changed. India was still a British colony. Tagore [the poet] explained the difference. "Those who live in England, far away from the East," he told the [British newspaper] *Manchester Guardian* of May 17, 1930, "have now got to realize that Europe has completely lost her former moral prestige in Asia. She is no longer regarded as the champion throughout the world of fair dealing and the exponent of high principle, but as the upholder of Western race supremacy and the exploiter of those outside her own borders.

"For Europe this is, in actual fact, a great moral defeat that has happened. Even though Asia is still physically weak and unable to protect herself from aggression where her vital interests are menaced, nevertheless she can now afford to look down on Europe where before she looked up." He attributed the achievement in India to Mahatma Gandhi.

Gandhi did two things in 1930: he made the British people aware that they were cruelly subjugating India, and he gave Indians the conviction that they could, by lifting their heads and straightening their spines, lift the yoke from their shoulders. After that, it was inevitable that Britain should some day refuse to rule India and that India should some day refuse to be ruled.

The British beat the Indians with batons and rifle butts. The Indians neither cringed nor complained nor retreated. That made England powerless and India invincible.

EVENT 7 **Mahatma Gandhi's Salt March Strikes a Blow for Indian Independence: March 1930**

The Salt March Spawns a Larger Independence Movement

by N.B. Parulekar

In the following eyewitness account taken from a May 1930 issue of the *New Republic*, Indian journalist N.B. Parulekar takes a closer look at the powerful effect Mahatma Gandhi's Salt March had on the Indians and the British in March and April of 1930. Warned in advance of Gandhi's proposed civil disobedience to break the Salt Laws, the British sent police to the seashore to train for the coming event, but in the end, the passive resisters were more than they could handle. Manufacture of contraband salt spread rapidly across India. In one case on the sands of Chaupati, nearly two hundred thousand demonstrators gathered for public meetings. Afterward, participants broke the Salt Laws by filling brass pots full of forbidden seawater to evaporate into salt, which in Bombay eventually dropped the price of salt in half.

The Salt March dramatically increased the momentum of the independence movement. According to Parulekar, it was a catalyst to further attacks on British authority, as in the direct boycott of government officials and the police. Since Indians typically helped run the British government and worked in the police force under British command, many Indians found themselves in a precarious position.

N.B. Parulekar, "India: A Nation on Strike: An Eyewitness Report of the Passive Revolt," *The New Republic*, vol. 63, May 28, 1930, pp. 39–40.

One newspaper reported that nearly eight hundred Indians had resigned their government jobs as a result, collapsing operations in those areas overnight. In one example, villagers refused to let an armed police party draw water or purchase food.

Overall, the Salt March was a major turning point in India's struggle for independence. To Gandhi's surprise, both men and women became involved. Participants ranged from professionals such as doctors and writers to college students and housewives, to indentured laborers and the poor. The march also exposed British injustice to the rest of the world, as journalists from all over reported India's fight for basic rights. That millions of passive resisters endured punishment and injury willingly, and did not retaliate with violence, was Gandhi's "most remarkable achievement," Parulekar reported. No government could withstand that kind of resistance for long.

N.B. Parulekar received his Ph.D. from the School of Journalism at Columbia University, New York, and was a regular contributor to leading U.S. periodicals. In 1932, he founded the Indian newspaper, *Daily Sakal*, which gave its support to Gandhi's mass movement. He was highly acclaimed in Indian journalism and by readers.

An Eyewitness Report of the Passive Revolt

Before Mahatma Gandhi made his march to the sea, the police began rehearsing possible methods of dealing with his troop of passive resisters. I am told that a little play was staged by the seashore in the Gujerath. One policeman, who played the part of Gandhi, dipped a pot of water from the Indian Ocean. At this a second policeman cried, "Halt!" "I refuse to obey," answered the first. His fellow officer then took him by the hand and prevented him from going farther. This pleasant comedy—which, I am told, was repeated in other training camps for the police—was supposed to prepare them for all possible eventualities. But when the passive-resistance movement actually began, it proved far beyond their powers to subdue.

At Bhimrad, for example, 322 men headed by Ramdas Gandhi, the son of the Mahatma, went to the seashore early one morning and collected fifty-five maunds (over 4400 pounds) of salt. Huge gunnysacks were filled, and every person carried a bag of twenty to thirty pounds. The police arrested Ramdas Gandhi and four others, declared the salt contraband and confiscated it. But the other 317 volunteers lay flat on the ground, refusing to part with their goods, and there followed a tug-of-war between the police and the passive resisters. At the rate of fifteen minutes for each volunteer, it would have taken several days to seize the entire stock. Realizing the futility of the performance, the police left the place with their five prisoners and a few hundred pounds of salt, as much as they could carry. The rest remained with the volunteers, who parceled it into two-ounce packages. Later on these were sold in the bazaars of Surat, Ahmedabad, and other places like peanuts in the streets of New York.

In Bombay, a thousand volunteers began selling salt. It has been a daily practice for several thousand men and women to go to the seaside as religiously as they would go to the Ganges [River], and to bring home pots filled with sea water, this being a breach of the salt law. The passive resisters hold public meetings on the sands of Chaupati, where nearly two hundred thousand have sometimes assembled. The members of the audience carry brass pots, which are filled with sea water after the meeting is over and carried home. Within one week from the starting of *Satyagraha*, the price of salt in Bombay had gone down by half. [*Satyagraha*: Concept of truth and love developed by Gandhi, and force behind the civil disobedience movement.]

Why Break the Salt Laws?

If the salt law was chosen by Gandhi as the first point of attack in his campaign of civil disobedience, it was because salt, though a common necessity, is a government monopoly . . . with a tax amounting to 2000 percent of the actual cost of production. This works as a poll tax on all, including women, invalids, and children. The salt regulations, moreover, are easy to break. [The Salt Act of 1882 regulated possession and manufacture of salt.] No government can successfully prevent an insurgent population of many millions from collecting, manufacturing or selling salt from a coastline of more than three thousand miles—to say nothing of guarding the innumerable salt deposits in the interior where people can help themselves.

Mahatma Gandhi's aim is to nullify British authority by breaking the British-made laws one by one without . . . violating ethical obligations. Let me quote a few reports from Indian newspapers to indicate the drift of the movement: "Nearly 800 *patels* [members of Hindu caste], or village officers, have resigned from as many villages, with the result that the [British] government administration in those villages has collapsed. "It is a sin on the part of village officials," writes one of them in his resignation, "to continue to cooperate with a government which has lost its head and persecutes its people inconsiderately."

Further Attack on British Authority

[Another newspaper reports] "The social boycott against government officials continues. An armed police party came in the morning and had to go without food and water, as the villagers refused to give even a rope to draw water. A Rajput [member of Hindu caste] in the village gave them a vessel. A meeting of the villagers was immediately called, and the vessel was taken back with cries of '*Bande mataram.*' [Hindu mantra and early nationalist anthem.] The collector of Kaira, who is the highest government officer in the district, could not purchase even tooth paste from the bazaars."

"Mr. Broker, the [British] crown prosecutor of Ahmedabad, has suspended his practice and has asked Mahatma Gandhi for orders as to where and when he should join him." "A student procession will parade through the town tomorrow morning, preaching the boycott of British goods. Sixteen students were expelled from the hostel for attending public meetings and for refusing to salute the Union Jack [British flag]." "Four Calcutta colleges," says another message, "are emptied of their students, who have organized . . . picketing at the college doors. In the evening, ten thousand people, mostly students, gathered in a public meeting, which was charged by the police. Several of the demonstrators were injured. A bonfire of foreign goods [foreign in India generally means British] was staged by the students. It included even handkerchiefs, pencils, and cigarettes."

The boycott of British goods is spreading rapidly. The merchants' associations of Bombay, Ahmedabad, Lahore, Amritsar, Nagpur, Madras, and many other large cities in India have passed resolutions prohibiting their members from dealing in foreign cloth, particularly British cloth. Those who defy the resolutions are penalized; in some cases they are fined as much as 1000 rupees, in addition to being expelled from the association. Even doctors have joined the movement. The All-India Medical Conference has adopted resolutions urging medical practitioners to prescribe drugs of Indian manufacture.

Indian Women Take on New Role

What is still more significant is the part played by women in the national agitation. A good many of them, after being so long confined within the four walls of their homes, have cast off their bonds and are taking an unusually large share in the program of passive resistance. They lead processions, speak from platforms, and organize women's volunteer corps. Their enthusiasm for political action, their sense of liberty, and their consciousness of women's role in the national life are remarkable, particularly in a country where orthodoxy still limits their activities. This awakening of the Indian women was so sudden, so spontaneous, and so independent of convention, that even the shrewdest politicians were taken by surprise. Gandhi, in his first outline, had not taken them into account; but now he had to revise his plan, call in a special conference of women, and entrust them with what may be called a fighting program. In particular they are to have

Indian women march to the sea in defiance of their country's salt laws.

charge of the boycott against foreign cloth and the picketing of liquor shops.

Indian Politics in Disarray

Party politics in India has almost ceased to exist; the public feels itself attuned to something else, something which it considers to be more expressive of its own feelings. The Moderates [Indians] have lost whatever influence they once possessed. It is true that Sir Chimanlal Setlwad, Sir Pheroz Sethna, and other Moderate leaders—they are also known as Liberals—tried to promote an intense propaganda to support Dominion status [self-rule] and the proposed round-table conference [in London to discuss possible constitutional reform] but on several occasions when they tried to hold meetings, the audience hooted them down and passed from the same platform resolutions demanding independence as the immediate goal of India. There is scarcely a large city in India where the Moderates have a chance of public hearing. They have plenty of money, but no men.

The fact is—and I suppose the [British] officials are more aware of it than anyone else—that the government, in the last resort, has no allies except its own troops. India . . . has the air of a country under military occupation. Everywhere there are soldiers, policemen, and armed auxiliaries. The railway lines, the law courts, the seashore places, the traveling officials—all are guarded. Recently, I passed through the Balkans and the countries of the Near East, which are known as the sore spots of the modern world. The present military look of India surpasses them all.

Meanwhile, what is the government's method of combating the campaign of civil disobedience? It can, of course, fall back on its cannon, but there is not room enough in the jails to accommodate all the offenders. Under these circumstances, it has adopted the policy of arresting only a select few—yet even so, and even though the mass of passive resisters is still at large, there must be several thousand people behind British bars.

Pundit Gaya Sahai Chaube, of Lucknow, was arrested for manufacturing salt. The sub-inspector of police deposed that the accused boiled water strained out of saline earth on . . . [a] pan before a gathering of 2,500. Yet the prosecution could not find another witness. Mr. Abid Ali of Bombay was charged with the same offense. The magistrate asked him whether he wished to make a statement. He answered, "I do not recognize the British government, much less this court, and therefore you will not consider me uncivil if I do not make any statement." The arrested men refuse to give their names, answer any questions, or defend themselves in the court. They may be charged with membership in an unlawful assembly, sedition, contempt of court, breaking the salt law, and with other possible offenses. But their attitude is consistently the same: they refuse to recognize the government.

Gandhi's Ultimate Goal: India's Independence

In other words, what Gandhi and his followers are aiming at is nothing less than an outlawry of the British regime in India—and this with the help of the civil population exclusively. No government on earth, far less an alien government such as that of Great Britain in India, can hope to maintain its law and order when the whole population refuses to obey it. That millions of people should be willing to suffer punishment and physical injuries—that they should remain peaceful even when they have a chance to retaliate—is Gandhi's most remarkable achievement. There may in the future be riots, bloodshed, and public violence at certain spots—India is after all a country larger than western Europe—but the loss of *life* will be infinitesimally small compared with what would surely have occurred in the absence of passive resistance.

Just as industrial workers may hope to have their grievances redressed by peaceful strike and arbitration, instead of . . . destroying the industry and its management, so also, says Mahatma Gandhi, a nation may go on strike. By this means it may get rid of a government that tries to perpetuate itself by force. If a whole people refuses to pay taxes or obey the laws—if it abstains from assisting the authorities in every possible manner—then the government will be forced to surrender as a government. Its authority will pass automatically to the leaders of the people. If this happens, so Gandhi says, India will have advanced the cause of world peace by showing in her own example the power of a peaceful revolt.

EVENT **8** Adolf Hitler Becomes Chancellor of Germany: January 30, 1933

Hitler Becomes Chancellor: A Recipe for Disaster

by Ian Kershaw

In the following article, excerpted from *Hitler, 1889–1936: Hubris*, author Ian Kershaw transports readers to Berlin, where, in 1933, Adolf Hitler's appointment as chancellor of Germany first made its dramatic impact on the German people. Many applauded and welcomed Hitler's chancellorship, according to Kershaw. The gushing excitement of a schoolteacher over Hitler's appointment was typical of others, who, like her, rooted in middle-class national-conservative beliefs, longed for Germany's renewal (the Great Depression had been hard on Germany). Of the churches, many Protestants were optimistic about the recent turn of events, seeing the potential of Hitler's influence on the nation's moral rejuvenation. And then there were the Nazis themselves, who envisioned great "opportunities for prosperity, advancement, and power" under Hitler's rule.

On the other hand, millions of Germans viewed the event without such enthusiasm, ranging from feelings of fear and anxiety to attitudes of "illusory optimism" and indifference, according to Kershaw. For some, Hitler did not represent a threat at all, and they continued about their business in seeming apathy—and denial. Catholics, however, were uneasy with the Nazis' anti-Christian conduct, and Protestants remained divided for and against Nazi rule, although churches in general ultimately made political compromises that put them on the defensive. Then there were the immediate victims of the new regime, those who suddenly found themselves un-

---

der political persecution, a situation that would become increasingly violent over time as Hitler's power solidified.

As to how Hitler gained control over the German people, Kershaw points out that after the army gave its unreserved allegiance to Hitler, the dictatorship became firmly entrenched. This, along with the effects of the Great Depression, the German people's growing discontent with government under democracy, the fear of Marxism, and the weakness of the established elite class, which used Hitler's mass appeal for its own revolutionary aims but lost to Hitler's dominance, all contributed to an event that would change the face of Germany forever. After President Paul von Hindenburg's death in 1934, Hitler assumed full power and millions of Germans fell under the spell of what Kershaw calls Hitler's "heroic, almost messianic qualities."

Ian Kershaw, who has been a lecturer, educator, and writer of history since 1968, is currently professor and chair of modern history at the University of Sheffield in England. As a scholar of modern and medieval history, he has written extensively, in particular, on Hitler's and the Nazi Party's rise to power during the 1930s. His work *Hitler, 1936–1945: Nemesis* (2000), the second volume of the book from which this article is excerpted, earned Kershaw the acclaimed British Academy Book Award in 2001. As a biographer of Hitler, he is credited with explaining how Germany could become so enamored with Hitler and what in particular made his rise to power possible.

> 'It can't be denied: he has grown. Out of the demagogue and party leader, the fanatic and agitator, the true statesman . . . seems to be developing.'
>
> Diary entry of the writer Erich Ebermayer, 21 March 1933

> 'What the old parliament and parties did not accomplish in sixty years, your statesmanlike foresight has achieved in six months.'
>
> Letter to Hitler from Cardinal Michael von Faulhaber, 24 July 1933

> 'In nine months, the genius of your leadership and the ideals which you have newly placed before us have succeeded in creating, from a people inwardly torn apart and without hope, a united Reich.'
>
> Franz von Papen, 14 November 1933, speaking on behalf of the members of the Reich Government

> Hitler is Reich Chancellor! And what a cabinet!!! One such as we did not dare to dream of in July. Hitler, [Alfred] Hugenberg, [Franz] Seldte, Papen!!! A large part of my German hopes are attached to each. National Socialist drive, German National reason, . . . and—not forgotten by us—Papen [former chancellor]. It is so unimaginably wonderful. . . . What an achievement by [President Paul von] Hindenburg!

This was the ecstatic response of Hamburg schoolteacher Luise Solmitz to the dramatic news of Hitler's appointment to the Chancellorship on 30 January 1933. Like so many who had found their way to Hitler from middle-class, national-conservative backgrounds, she had wavered the previous autumn when she thought he was slipping under the influence of radical socialist tendencies in the party. Now that Hitler was in office, but surrounded by her trusted champions of the conservative Right, heading a government of 'national concentration', her joy was unbounded. The national renewal she longed for could now begin. Many, outside the ranks of diehard Nazi followers, their hopes and ideals invested in the Hitler cabinet, felt the same way.

But millions did not. Fear, anxiety, alarm, implacable hostility, illusory optimism at the regime's early demise, and bold defiance intermingled with apathy, scepticism, condescension towards the presumed inability of the new Chancellor and his Nazi colleagues in the cabinet—and indifference.

Reactions varied according to political views and personal disposition. 'What will this government do?' asked Julius Leber, SPD [Social Democratic Party] Reichstag deputy, before, his immunity ignored, being taken into custody the very night after Hitler's accession to power after being beaten up by a group of Nazi thugs. 'We know their aims. Nobody knows what their next measures will be. The dangers are enormous. But the firmness of German workers is unshakeable. We don't fear these men. We are determined to take up the struggle.'. . .

Religious Reaction

The leadership of the Zentrum [the Catholic party] concentrated on seeking assurances that unconstitutional measures would be avoided. The Catholic hierarchy remained reserved, its disquiet about Hitler and the anti-Christian tendencies of his movement unchanged. Influenced by years of warnings from their clergy, the Catholic population were apprehensive and uncertain. Among many Protestant church-goers there was, according to the later recollections of one pastor, a great optimism that national renewal would bring with it inner, moral revitalization: 'It is as if the wing of a great turn of fate is fluttering above us. There was to be a new start.' The Land Bishop of Württemberg, Theophil Wurm, soon to run into conflict with the new rulers, also recalled how the Protestant Church welcomed the Hitler Chancellorship since the National Socialists [Hitler's party] had resolutely fought Marxist 'anti-Church agitation', and now offered new hope for the future and the expectation of a 'favourable impact on the entire people'. One of the leading Protestant theologians, Karl Barth, later dismissed from his Chair at Bonn University for his hostility to the 'German Christians' (the nazified wing of the Protestant Church), took a different view, airly dismissing any major significance in Hitler's appointment. 'I don't think that this will signify the start of great new things in any direction at all,' he wrote to his mother on 1 February 1933.

Apathy Among Many

Many ordinary people, after what they had gone through in the Depression, were simply apathetic at the news that Hitler was Chancellor. According to the British Ambassador in Berlin, Horace Rumbold, people throughout the country 'took the news phlegmatically'. Those in provincial Germany who were not Nazi fanatics or committed opponents often shrugged their shoulders and carried on with life, doubtful that yet another change of government would bring any improvement. Some thought that Hitler would not even be as long in office as [former Chancellor] Schleicher, and that his popularity would slump as soon as disillusionment set in on account of the emptiness of Nazi promises. But perceptive critics of Hitler were able to see that, now he enjoyed the prestige of the Chancellorship, he could swiftly break down much of the scepticism and win great support by successfully tackling mass unemployment—something which none of his predecessors had come close to achieving. . . .

Nazi Celebration

For the Nazis themselves, of course, 30 January 1933 was the day they had dreamed about, the triumph they had fought for, the opening of the portals to the brave new world—and the start of what many hoped would be opportunities for prosperity, advancement, and power. Wildly cheering crowds accompanied Hitler on his way back to the Kaiserhof [Hotel] after his appointment with Hindenburg. 'Now we've got there,' Hitler declared, carried away with the euphoria around him, as he stepped out of the lift on the first floor of the Kaiserhof to be greeted, alongside [Joseph] Goebbels and other Nazi leaders, by waiters and chambermaids, all anxious to shake his hand. By seven o'clock that evening Goebbels had improvised a torchlight procession of marching SA [storm troop] and SS [protection squad] men through the centre of Berlin that lasted beyond midnight. He wasted no time in exploiting the newly available facilities of state radio to provide a stirring commentary. Goebbels claimed a million men had taken part. The Nazi press halved the number. The British Ambassador estimated a maximum figure of some 50,000. His military attaché thought there were around 15,000. Whatever the numbers, the spectacle was an unforgettable one—exhilarating and intoxicating for Nazi followers, menacing for those at home and abroad who feared the consequences of Hitler in power. One fifteen-year-old girl was mesmerized by what she saw. For Melita Maschmann, the marching columns gave 'mag-

Hitler, shown here saluting his troops, quickly transformed Germany after becoming chancellor in 1933.

ical splendour' to the idea of the 'national community' which had fascinated her. Afterwards, she could scarcely wait to join the BDM (Bund deutscher Mädel, the German Girls' League, the female section of the Hitler Youth organization). Her idealism was shared by many, particularly among the young, who saw the dawn of a new era symbolized in the spectacular torchlight procession through the centre of Berlin.

The seemingly endless parade was watched from his window in the Wilhelmstrabet by Reich President Hindenburg. Berliners later joked that the President liked torchlight processions because he was allowed to stay up late when they took place. There was respectful shouts when the procession passed him by. But when the marchers came to the window a little farther on, where Hitler was standing, the respect gave way to wild acclaim. For Papen, a few feet behind Hitler, it symbolized the transition 'from a moribund regime to the new revolutionary forces'.

The day of Hitler's appointment to the Chancellorship became immediately stylized in Nazi mythology as the 'day of the national uprising'. Hitler even contemplated—so, at least, he claimed later—changing the calendar (as the French revolutionaries had done) to mark the beginning of a 'new world order'. At the same time he—and other Nazi spokesmen generally followed suit—avoided the term 'seizure of power', with its putschist connotations, and preferred the more descriptive 'takeover of power' to underline the formal legality of his accession to the highest office of government. Power had indeed not been 'seized'. It had been handed to Hitler, who had been appointed Chancellor by the Reich President in the same manner as had his immediate predecessors. Even so, the orchestrated ovations, which put Hitler himself and other party bosses into a state of ecstasy, signalled that this was no ordinary transfer of power. And almost overnight, those who had misunderstood or misinterpreted the momentous nature of the day's events would realize how wrong they had been. After 30 January 1933, Germany would never be the same again.

That historic day was an end and a beginning. It denoted the expiry of the unlamented Weimar Republic and the culminating point of the comprehensive state crisis that had brought its demise. At the same time Hitler's appointment as Chancellor marked the beginning of the process which was to lead into the abyss of war and genocide, and bring about Germany's own destruction as a nation-state. It signified the start of that astonishingly swift jettisoning of constraints on inhumane behaviour whose path ended in Auschwitz, Treblinka, Sobibor, Majdanek, and the other death camps whose names are synonymous with the horror of Nazism. . . .

What made Hitler's triumph possible were important strands of continuity in German political culture stretching back beyond the First World War—chauvinistic nationalism, imperialism, racism, anti-Marxism, glorification of war, the placing of order above freedom, caesaristic attractions of strong authority are some of them—as well as the specific and more short-term consequences of the multi-layered crises that afflicted Weimar democracy from the start. But if such continuities helped 'make Hitler possible', and if his triumph can at least partially be explained by his unique capacity in 1933 to bind together for a time all the strands of continuity with 'old Germany', the following twelve years would see these elements of continuity exploited, warped and distorted out of all recognition by the ever intensifying radicalism of the regime, then ultimately broken in the maelstrom of defeat and destruction in 1945 that Hitler's rule had produced.

The Rapid Takeover of Political and Social Structures

The rapidity of the transformation that swept over Germany between Hitler's takeover of power on 30 January 1933 and its crucial consolidation and extension at the beginning of August 1934, after Reich President Hindenburg's death [due to illness] and following close on the major crisis of the 'Röhm affair' [Hitler accused the SA leader of treason and had him shot], was astounding for contemporaries and is scarcely less astonishing in retrospect. It was brought about by a combination of pseudo-legal measures, terror, manipulation—and willing collaboration. Within a month, civil liberties—as protected under the Weimar Constitution—had been extinguished. Within two months, with most active political opponents either imprisoned or fleeing the country, the Reichstag surrendered its powers, giving Hitler control of the legislature. Within four months the once powerful trade unions were dissolved. In less than six months, all opposition parties had been suppressed or gone into voluntary liquidation, leaving the NSDAP [Nazi Party] as the only remaining party. In January 1934, the sovereignty of the Länder—already in reality smashed the previous March—was formally abolished. Then, in the summer, the growing threat from within Hitler's own movement was ruthlessly eliminated in the 'Night of the Long Knives' on 30 June 1934. [At least seventy-seven party members alleged to have plotted against Hitler were murdered.]

By this time, almost all organizations, institutions, professional and representative bodies, clubs, and societies had long since rushed to align themselves with the new regime. 'Tainted' remnants of pluralism and democracy were rapidly removed, nazified structures and mentalities adopted. This process of 'coordination' (*Gleichschaltung*) was for the most part undertaken voluntarily and with alacrity.

Difficulty with the Christian Churches

The Christian churches were exceptions to the process. Attempts to 'coordinate' the divided Protestant Church caused great conflict and had eventually to be abandoned. No attempt was even made to alter the organizational framework of the Catholic Church. The lasting tension and frequent clashes between the churches—especially the Catholic Church—and the regime in the following years were rooted in alternative sources of loyalty which the Christian denominations continued to command. But the political compromises which each of them made with the new rules in the first months nevertheless pushed them on to the defensive, forcing them to become largely reactive and inward-looking.

The Allegiance of the Army

The army, too, remained 'uncoordinated', its officer corps still largely national-conservative, not Nazi. Without the army's backing, Hitler could not rule. But however contemptuous many of the reactionary and conservative officers, often from aristocratic backgrounds, were of the upstart former corporal now running the government, his offer of 'everything for the armed forces', and his readiness to eradicate those forces in his own movement that threatened the army's position, won him their support. The oath of allegiance which the army swore to Hitler personally at the death of the Reich President and war-hero Field Marshal Hindenburg on 2 August 1934 symbolically marked its full acceptance of the new order. With this act, Hitler's dictatorship was firmly established.

The Balance of Power That Led to Hitler's Victory

The speed of the transformation, and the readiness of the army and other traditionally powerful groups to put themselves at the service of the new regime, derived in no small measure from the conditions in which Hitler took power. The weakness of the established élites of the 'old order' had eventually led to Hitler's appointment to the Chancellorship. The traditional power-groups had helped undermine and destroy the democracy they so detested. But they had been incapable of imposing the type of counter-revolution they had wanted. Hitler had needed them in order to gain power. But they had needed Hitler, too, to provide mass support for their intended counter-revolution. This was the basis of the 'entente' that put Hitler in the Chancellor's seat.

The balance of power in the 'entente' between Hitler and his conservative partners was nevertheless tilted from the outset towards the new Chancellor. In particular, the anxiety of the army to avoid civil strife and to attain domestic peace as a prerequisite of remilitarization assured its cooperation and willingness to support Hitler's brutal deployment of the power of the state. For only Hitler, and the huge—if potentially unstable—mass movement he headed, could ensure control of the streets and bring about the 'destruction of Marxism', the basis of the desired counter-revolution. Yet precisely this dependence on Hitler and eagerness to back the most ruthless measures adopted in the early weeks and months of the new regime guaranteed that the weakness of the traditional élite groups would become laid bare in the years to come as the intended counter-revolution gave way to the attempted Nazi racial revolution in Europe and opened the path to world conflagration and genocide.

Remarkable in the seismic upheavals of 1933–34 was not how much, but how little, the new Chancellor needed to do to bring about the extension and consolidation of his power. Hitler's dictatorship was made as much as by others as by himself. As the 'representative figure' of the 'national renewal', Hitler could for the most part function as activator and enabler of the forces he had unleashed, authorizing and legitimating actions taken by others now rushing to implement what they took to be his wishes. 'Working towards the Führer' functioned as the underlying maxim of the regime from the outset.

Hitler was, in fact, in no position to act as an outright dictator when he came to office on 30 January 1933. As long as Hindenburg lived, there was a potential rival source of loyalty—not least for the army. But by summer 1934, when he combined the headship of state with the leadership of government, his power had effectively shed formal constraints on its usage. And, by then, the personality cult built around Hitler had reached new levels of idolatry and made millions of new concerns as the 'people's chancellor'—as propaganda had styled him—came to be seen as a national, not merely party, leader. Disdain and detestation for a parliamentary system generally perceived to have failed miserably had resulted in willingness to entrust monopoly control over the state to a leader claiming a unique sense of mission and invested by his mass following with heroic, almost messianic, qualities. Conventional forms of government were, as a consequence, increasingly exposed to the arbitrary inroads of personalized power. It was a recipe for disaster.

EVENT 8 **Adolf Hitler Becomes Chancellor of Germany: January 30, 1933**

Europe Reacts to Hitler's Rise

by the *Literary Digest*

Recognizing the significance of Adolf Hitler's rise to power in Germany on January 30, 1933, and his potential threat to Europe, the press reacted immediately. Following is an article excerpted from the February 1933 issue of the periodical, the *Literary Digest*, summarizing the reactions of French, British, and German journalists. Some appeared to be optimistic, more impressed it seemed with the greatness of Hitler's achievement and his similarities to Germany's great leaders of the past. More, however, seemed to understand that Hitler's appointment as chancellor by German President Paul von Hindenburg meant trouble ahead.

Mention is also made of Hitler's first official act to dissolve the Reichstag, Germany's parliament, and the call for a new election on March 5. This was crucial to Hitler's chancellorship since Germany's Weimar constitution required that he also be elected. Later, Hitler would effectively tip the scale in his favor by fabricating a communist plot just days before the election, after the Reichstag mysteriously caught fire. A revolutionary sweep of government would result in the imprisonment of many communists and social democrats, removing much of his opposition. One journalist correctly predicted this, suggesting that Hitler's rise would be a "mortal blow" to the Weimar constitution and parliamentary government.

What appears to be lacking in the press' assessment of Hitler's rise is any mention of the harm that the Nazi regime would bring to the Jewish population in Germany and elsewhere, although one journalist insightfully points out that anti-Jewish pogroms would be

"What Hitler Rule Means to Europe," *Literary Digest*, vol. 115, February 11, 1933, p. 12.

a definite outcome. A follow-up article published by the *Literary Digest*, February 23, 1933, tells of a Jewish exodus from Germany following Hitler's appointment, but apparently, a large number remained behind believing that President Paul von Hindenburg would offset Hitler's anti-Semitism.

The weekly U.S. magazine, the *Literary Digest*, was first published in 1890 by Isaac Funk and Adam Wagnalls. Highly popular, the magazine drew its news impartially from newspaper reports, and thus it was often used as a current events source in high schools and colleges. In 1921, it had a circulation of 1.2 million, but in the 1930s, interest waned and it was eventually bought out by *Time* magazine in 1938.

"Whether or not Hitler turns out to be a clown or a faker, those by his side now, and those who may replace him later, are not figures to be joked with."

With this grim thought, the semiofficial Paris *Temps* greets the accession of "handsome Adolf" Hitler to the Chancellorship in Germany. The event, it adds, is "of greater importance than any event since the fall of the Hohenzollerns [ruling family of Germany 1891–1918]."

In England, the Laborite *Daily Herald* declares solemnly that "with Hitler's appointment the way is prepared for the return of the ex-Kaiser [Wilhelm II]." But in sharp contrast the London *Daily Mail* remarks "it looks as if Germany has a stable Government at last."

Hitler's first official act on February 1 was to dissolve the Reichstag [parliament] under authority of a decree signed by President Paul von Hindenburg [who had appointed Hitler as chancellor], and to set a new general election for March 5.

Thus, in the seats of the mighty now flourishes the forty-four-year-old Austrian-born agitator of dark and flaming eyes. Of medium height, rather slender, with black hair, and a pale, sallow complexion, the press remind us again, he wears a toothbrush mustache, lets his hair fall over one brow, and affects a uniform on most occasions. He is "a natural orator who knows how to move the inarticulate mass and play upon popular resentments."

"The legacy which we take over is a fearful one," Hitler said on February 1 in his radio manifesto, signed by every member of his Cabinet and appealing to the German nation for support in the balloting on March 5 for a new Reichstag. "The task which we are called upon to solve is the most difficult ever put before German statesmen within the memory of man." But the confidence of himself and of his Cabinet is "boundless," for "we believe in our people and its imperishable worth." As quoted in the press, he went on:

"The National President, Field Marshal von Hindenburg, has summoned us with the command to bring to the nation the possibility of reconstruction by our unanimity. We appeal, therefore, to the German people to sign with us this deed of reconciliation.

The government of national resurrection wants to work, and it will work. It has not brought low the German nation in fourteen years, but it will lead it upward again. It is determined in four years to make good the wrongs of fourteen years.

But it can not submit the work of reconstruction to the approval of those who are to blame for the crash. The parties of Marxism and its abettors have had fourteen years in which to show their ability. The result is a field of ruins. Now, German people, give us a period of four years, and then judge us and give us your verdict. . . .

As regards foreign policy, the national government sees its highest mission in the maintenance of the vital rights and therewith restoration of the liberty of our people. While it is determined to put an end to the chaotic conditions in Germany, it will help to add a state of equal worth and, of course, equal rights to the community of nations. It is thereby filled with a sense of the greatness of its duty to stand up with this free and equal people for the preservation and strengthening of peace which the world needs to-day more than ever before. May the good-will of others aid us, in order that our most sincere wish for the welfare of Europe and, indeed, the world, be brought to fulfilment.

Great as is our love for our Army as the bearer of our arms and the symbol of our great past, yet we would be happy if the world, through limitation of armaments, would render increase of our own weapons nevermore necessary."

A Celebration First

What happened in Berlin on that night of portent, January 30, when a public celebration of a change of Chancellors was held for the first time in the history of the Republic, is dramatically portrayed in a Berlin copyrighted cable to the New York *Sun*, in which we read:

"At a lighted window in Bismarck's [former 1890 chancellor's] old room in the German chancellery, looking out on the Wilhelmstrasse, an old man [President Hindenburg], 220 pounds in weight, white-haired, and monumental, stood for four hours while between 30,000 and 40,000 yellow-clad members of the Nazi storm battalions and 2,000 Steel Helmet [a nationalistic organization] adherents, and a great number of common citizens filed by with torches in their hands.

Nearly all the marchers saluted the old man, who sometimes raised his hand or nodded in answer, occasionally wincing as a pitiless search-light fell full upon his serious face.

Once more Paul von Hindenburg, directing genius of the German armies in the World War, and now President of the Republic, was accepting the homage of his people at the cost of his slumber.

Meanwhile, a hundred yards farther on the south wing of the building, against the background of a lighted room with pale blue walls, was a second figure—that of the new Chancellor, Adolf Hitler, leader of the victorious National Socialists.

Drest in a frock coat and silhouetted against the light, he raised his hand a thousand times in the ancient Roman greeting which he has taken for his party salute.

Below, the streets were thronged with people cheering. Thus the man, who in the last fifteen years has never held a real job, and who a year ago was virtually without a country, was welcomed to the seat of Bismarck." [German chancellor 1871–1890.]

A Grave Assessment by the Press

How gravely affected the French and British are by Hitler's rise to power appears in additional cabled editorials to those cited above received from the European press by *The Literary Digest*. Dictatorship in Germany looms on the view of the Paris *Figaro*, which declares:

"The Weimar Constitution and parliamentarism has received a mortal blow. Participation of the Catholic party being withheld, handsome Adolf will undoubtedly make a play for dictatorial power, representing the gravest danger for France."

Redoubled vigilance on the part of France, says the *Ere Nouvelle*, "must now be the order with this new muddle entering into the already scrambled international situation." The *Echo de Paris* also sees storm-signals set for the Franco-German political area, and it points out:

Hitler comes to power at last just as our Socialists for the first time agree to cooperate in the Government. Manifestly things are moving in opposite directions in the two countries. "He, too, warns that Germany is headed straight for ultra-nationalism, perhaps even monarchy—and France for trouble."

A tone of dismay is heard in the comment of the Paris *Quotidien*, which marvels at the lightning change in the political front of Germany, as it observes:

The inevitable has arrived. It seemed impossible that monarchical Germany, for a few years in the ranks of the democratic nations, has for its head this hysterical confused demagog who succeeded in crystallizing the moral derangements of the German populace into a veritable Prussian discipline."

Few of the editorials from the English press cabled to *The Literary Digest* show the indignation of the London *Daily Telegraph*, which has little patience for the new German regime, as it asserts:

"The Chancellorship is filled by one whose astonishing mastery of the arts of demagogy has been devoted to organizing all of the contempt, disgust, sense of helplessness and humiliation with which millions regard the failure of parliamentary democracy.

Not from this Government will come the vaguely Socialistic, semi-Fascist dictatorship, the attack on banks and bourses, and the anti-Jewish pogroms, which are the nearest approach to anything definite in the Nazi outlook."

Nor does the London *Morning Post* see tranquillity ahead for Germany and the outside world, because Hitler's—

"Is not a Government which augurs well for internal peace. It is unfortunately, the kind which is apt to seek solution of its difficulties at home in adventures abroad."

But the London *News-Chronicle* foresees an alteration in the Hitler method, when it says:

"The Government's policy assuredly will not be the mixed grill of hatreds and prejudices which Hitler has been in the habit of serving to his admiring followers."

Among editorials cabled to *The Literary Digest* from the German press we find the Socialist *Vorwaerts*, one of Hitler's bitter opponents, girding its loins for future action, when it declares:

"Hitler's appointment initiates a new phase of the battle between democracy and Fascism, but by no means decides this struggle."

Outspoken concern is exprest by the extremely Nationalistic *Deutsche Zeitung*, which fears disaster unless the new Government succeeds, and it goes on:

"The road is now clear. The Hitler-Papen-Hugenberg Cabinet represents Germany's last reserve. If it fails, a catastrophe of gigantic dimensions is inevitable."

EVENT 9 President Roosevelt's Inauguration: March 4, 1933

Roosevelt's Inaugural Address

by Franklin D. Roosevelt

More than four thousand U.S. banks, fraught by panicked depositors, were in collapse the day President Franklin D. Roosevelt was inaugurated on March 4, 1933. In addition, more than 15 million people were out of work, and of those who held jobs, wages were 40 percent below 1929 levels. Was this the bottom? Americans had no way of knowing whether the economy would decline further or whether Roosevelt could turn the Great Depression around, but there was a definite air of hopefulness.

Roosevelt took the oath of office in the U.S. Senate chamber as the nation's thirty-second president and immediately launched into his inaugural speech. Outside the Capitol, a large crowd gathered for a glimpse of the new president, while millions more listened to his words on the radio. In the end, the speech would receive both national and international acclaim, and is still quoted to this day.

In short, the speech, excerpted here, was fearless. Roosevelt's words condemned the unscrupulous bankers and investment financiers behind the banking disaster, and more so, took the Great Depression to task, hinting at definite plans of attack. In particular, Roosevelt emphasized that restoration of the economy would require bold action, as in legislative action provided through the constitution, and action by the American people as one body united for the common good of all. Mostly, Roosevelt's speech rekindled the American spirit in one of the darkest hours of the Great Depression. It also established Roosevelt's reputation as a trusted leader, an important factor in promoting his antidepression legislation, the "New

Franklin D. Roosevelt, Inaugural Address, Washington, DC, March 4, 1933.

Deal," and later during World War II when his leadership was vital.

Franklin Delano Roosevelt (1882–1945) served three terms as president of the United States from 1933–1945.

I am certain that my fellow Americans expect that on my induction into the presidency, I will address them with a candor and a decision which the present situation of our nation impels. This is preeminently the time to speak the truth, the whole truth, frankly and boldly. Nor need we shrink from honestly facing conditions in our country to-day. This great nation will endure as it has endured, will revive and will prosper. So, first of all, let me assert my firm belief that the only thing we have to fear is fear itself— nameless, unreasoning, unjustified terror which paralyzes needed efforts to convert retreat into advance. In every dark hour of our national life, a leadership of frankness and vigor has met with that understanding and [the] support of the people themselves which is essential to victory. I am convinced that you will again give that support to leadership in these critical days.

In such a spirit, on my part and on yours, we face . . . common difficulties. They concern, thank God, only material things. Values have shrunken to fantastic levels; taxes have risen; our ability to pay has fallen; government of all kinds is faced by serious curtailment of income; the means of exchange are frozen in the currents of trade; the withered leaves of industrial enterprise lie on every side; farmers find no markets for their produce; the savings of many years in thousands of families are gone.

More important, a host of unemployed citizens face the grim problem of existence, and an equally great number toil with little return. Only a foolish optimist can deny the dark realities of the moment.

Unscrupulous Money Changers

Yet, our distress comes from no failure of substance. We are stricken by no plague of locusts. Compared with the perils which our forefathers conquered because they believed and were not afraid, we have still much to be thankful for. Nature still offers her bounty and human efforts have multiplied it. Plenty is at our doorstep, but a generous use of it languishes in the very sight of the supply. Primarily, this is because the rulers of the exchange of mankind's goods have failed, through their own stubbornness and their own incompetence; [they] have admitted their failure and abdicated. Practices of the unscrupulous money changers stand indicted in the court of public opinion, rejected by the hearts and minds of men.

True, they have tried, but their efforts have been cast in the pattern of an outworn tradition. Faced by failure of credit, they have proposed only the lending of more money. Stripped of the lure of profit by which to induce our people to follow their false leadership, they have resorted to exhortations, pleading tearfully for restored confidence. They know only the rules of a generation of self-seekers. They have no vision, and when there is no vision the people perish.

The Falsity of Material Wealth as a Standard of Success

The money changers have fled from their high seats in the temple of our civilization. We may now restore that temple to the ancient truths. The measure of the restoration lies in the extent to which we apply social values more noble than mere monetary profit.

Happiness lies not in the mere possession of money; it lies in the joy of achievement, in the thrill of creative effort. The joy and moral stimulation of work no longer must be forgotten in the mad chase of evanescent profits. These dark days will be worth all they cost us, if they teach us that our true destiny is not to be ministered unto but to minister to ourselves and to our fellow men.

Recognition of the falsity of material wealth as the standard of success goes hand in hand with the abandonment of the false belief that public office and high political position are to be valued only by the standards of pride of place and personal profit; and there must be an end to a conduct in banking and in business which too often has given to a sacred trust the likeness of callous and selfish wrongdoing. Small wonder that confidence languishes, for it thrives only on honesty, on honor, on the sacredness of obligations, on faithful protection, on unselfish performance; without them it can not live.

The Task Ahead Calls for Action

Restoration calls, however, not for changes in ethics alone. This Nation asks for action, and action now.

Our greatest primary task is to put people to work. This is no unsolvable problem if we face it wisely and courageously. It can be accomplished in part by direct recruiting by the Government itself, treating the task as we would treat the emergency of a war, but at the same time, through this employment, accomplishing greatly needed projects to stimulate and reorganize the use of our natural resources.

Hand in hand, with this we must frankly recognize the over-balance of population in our industrial centers and, by engaging on a national scale in a redistribution, endeavor to provide a better use of the land for those best fitted for the land. The task can be helped by definite efforts to raise the values of agricultural products, and with this, the power to purchase the output of our cities. It can be helped by preventing, realistically, the tragedy of the growing loss through foreclosure of our small homes and our farms. It can be helped by insistence that the federal, state, and local governments act forthwith on the demand that their costs be drastically reduced. It can be helped by the unifying of relief activities which to-day are often scattered, uneconomical, and unequal. It can be helped by national planning for, and supervision of, all forms of transportation; and of communications and other utilities which have a definitely public character. There are many ways in which it can be helped, but it can never be helped merely by talking about it. We must act and act quickly.

Finally, in our progress toward a resumption of work, we require two safeguards against a return of the evils of the old order; there must be a strict supervision of all banking and credits and investments; there must be an end to speculation with other people's money, and there must be provision for an adequate but sound currency.

There are the lines of attack. I shall presently urge upon a new Congress in special session detailed measures for their fulfillment, and I shall seek the immediate assistance of . . . several states.

Through this program of action, we address ourselves to putting our own national house in order and making income balance outgo. Our international trade relations, though vastly important, are in point of time and necessity secondary to the establishment of a sound national economy. I favor as a practical policy the putting of first things first. I shall spare no effort to restore world trade by international economic readjustment, but the emergency at home can not wait on that accomplishment.

The basic thought that guides these specific means of national recovery is not narrowly nationalistic. It is the insistence, as a first consideration, upon the interdependence of the various elements in . . . parts of the United States—a recognition of the old and permanently important manifestation of the American spirit of the pioneer. It is the way to recovery. It is the immediate way. It is the strongest assurance that the recovery will endure.

In the field of world policy, I would dedicate this nation to the policy of the good neighbor—the neighbor who resolutely respects himself and, because he does so, respects the rights of others—the neighbor who respects his obligations and respects the sanctity of his agreements in and with a world of neighbors.

If I read the temper of our people correctly, we now realize as we have never realized before our interdependence on each other; that we can not merely take, but we must give as well; that if we are to go forward, we must move as a trained and loyal army willing to sacrifice for the good of a common discipline, because without such discipline no progress is made, no leadership becomes effective. We are, I know, ready and willing to submit our lives and property to such discipline, because it makes possible a leadership which aims at a larger good. This I propose to offer, pledging that the larger purposes will bind . . . us all as a sacred obligation, with a unity of duty hitherto evoked only in time of armed strife.

With this pledge taken, I assume unhesitatingly the leadership of this great army of our people, dedicated to a disciplined attack upon our common problems.

Action Through the Constitution

Action in this image and to this end is feasible under the form of government which we have inherited from our ancestors. Our constitution is so simple and practical that it is possible always to meet extraordinary needs by changes in emphasis and arrangement without loss of essential form. That is why our constitutional system has proved itself the most superbly enduring political mechanism the modern world has produced. It has met every stress of vast expansion of territory, of foreign wars, of bitter internal strife, of world relations.

It is . . . hoped that the normal balance of executive and legislative authority may be wholly adequate to meet the unprecedented task before us. But it may be that an unprecedented demand and need for undelayed action may call for temporary departure from that normal balance of public procedure.

I am prepared under my constitutional duty to recommend the measures that a stricken nation in the midst of a stricken world may require. These measures, or such other measures as the Congress may build out of its experience and wisdom, I shall seek, within my constitutional authority, to bring to speedy adoption.

Facing the Crisis with Courage

But in the event that the Congress shall fail to take one of these two courses, and in the event that the national emergency is still critical, I shall not evade the clear course of duty that will then confront me. I shall ask the Congress for the one remaining instrument to meet the crisis—broad Executive power to wage a war against the emergency, as great as the power . . . given to me if we were in fact invaded by a foreign foe.

For the trust reposed in me, I will return the courage and the devotion that befit the time. I can do no less.

We face the arduous days that lie before us in the warm courage of the national unity; with the clear consciousness of seeking old and precious moral values; with the clean satisfaction that comes from the stern performance of duty by old and young alike. We aim at the assurance of a rounded and permanent national life.

We do not distrust the future of essential democracy. The people of the United States have not failed. In their need they have registered a mandate that they want direct, vigorous action. They have asked for discipline and direction under leadership. They have made me the present instrument of their wishes. In the spirit of the gift I take it.

In this dedication of a nation we humbly ask the blessing of God. May He protect each and every one of us. May He guide me in the days to come.

EVENT **9** **President Roosevelt's Inauguration: March 4, 1933**

FDR's Inaugural Launches a "New Deal"

by Frederick Lewis Allen

Accepting the nomination for president at the U.S. Democratic convention in 1932, Franklin D. Roosevelt declared a "new deal" for the American people, a campaign promise of depression relief that would carry through to his election in March 1933. Precisely how the New Deal would deliver the nation out of the Great Depression was somewhat vague, but once begun, the day after Roosevelt's inauguration, the role of government changed significantly. The federal government became immediately involved in the nation's financial security, of which the first order of business was the collapse of the banking system.

As banks across the country began shutting their doors in February 1933, depositors panicked and rushed to withdraw their funds, which only exacerbated the problem. In the following selection, Frederick Lewis Allen demonstrates how Roosevelt's inaugural address not only restored the confidence of Americans but also infused new energy into the chambers of the nation's lawgivers, the Congress. In a burst of legislative activity the day after his inauguration, Roosevelt and Congress tackled the banking crisis with swiftness, zeal, and determination. Roosevelt's bold, immediate handling of the banking problem helped relax the pent-up tension of all involved, according to Allen. Americans reacted to the president's declaration of a bank holiday with utter relief that the crisis was finally "out in the

---

Frederick Lewis Allen, *Since Yesterday: The 1930s in America, September 3, 1929–September 3, 1939*. New York: Harper & Brothers, 1939.

open." Although not all New Deal legislation would prove as successful, Roosevelt's inaugural call to action gave the New Deal in its early stages an edge up and a "brilliant beginning."

Frederick Lewis Allen was educated at Harvard University. He was a freelance writer and editor for *Atlantic Monthly, Century*, and *Harper's*. He also contributed to various other periodicals, including the *New Yorker.* He is best known for his work as editor of *Harper's* and for his writing of a series of informal but well-crafted histories that focus on the general trends in American culture.

Saturday, March 4, 1933.

Turn on the radio. It's time for the inauguration. There is a tension in the air today—a sense of momentousness and of expectation. When you went downtown this morning you found the banks shut; if you lived in New York State or in Illinois this may have been your first inkling of the general bank closing, since the closing orders in those states had come too late for the early editions of the morning papers of March 4. On the door of each bank was pasted a little typewritten notice that it had been closed at the Governor's order; people by twos and threes went up and read the sign and walked away. Your first thought, perhaps, was that you had only a little money in the house—five dollars, was it? ten dollars?—and you wondered how you would manage when this was used up, and what would happen next. Then you began to realize the significance of this financial stoppage.

Well, it's come at last, you thought. Here is that day of doom that people have been dreading. Just now it isn't so bad; there is a tingle of excitement, the sort of thrill you get from a three-alarm fire. But what next? This may be only the beginning of the crack-up. The one thing you want to hear, that everybody wants to hear, is the inaugural address. All over the country people are huddled round their radios, wondering what Roosevelt's answer to disaster will be.

Here's the voice of a radio reporter describing the preparations for the inauguration ceremony at the east front of the Capitol in Washington—the notables coming to their places on the platform, the dense crowds flooding the Capitol square below under a chill, cloudy sky. The reporter is talking with all the synthetic good cheer of his kind—bearing down hard on the note of optimism, in fact, for he knows that worried and frightened people are listening to him. He describes [President Herbert] Hoover coming alone, gravely, to his place on the platform; then Roosevelt coming up a ramp on the arm of his son James. The ceremony begins. You hear Chief Justice Hughes administer the oath of office; you hear Roosevelt's reply, phrase by phrase, uttered clearly and firmly. Then comes the inaugural.

Action, Action, Action

The new President's voice is resolute. It comes into your living room sharply.

"President Hoover, Mr. Chief Justice, my friends," the voice begins. "This is a day of national consecration, and I am certain that my fellow Americans expect that on my induction into the Presidency I will address them with a candor and a decision which the present situation of the nation impels. This is preeminently the time to speak the truth, frankly and boldly. Nor need we shrink from honestly facing conditions in our country today. This great nation will endure as it has endured, will revive and will prosper. So, first of all, let me assert my firm belief that the only thing we have to fear is fear itself—nameless, unreasoning, unjustified terror which paralyzes needed efforts to convert retreat into advance."

This doesn't sound like "prosperity is just around the corner" talk. It sounds like real confidence.

The voice goes on to blame "the rulers of the exchange of mankind's goods" for the troubles of the country. "True, they have tried, but their efforts have been cast in the pattern of an outworn tradition. . . . The money changers have fled from their high seats in the temple of our civilization." Through the radio comes a burst of applause: after the bank smash-ups and scandals, this condemnation of the big financiers expresses the mood of millions of Americans.

The voice speaks of the primary need of putting people to work; of the need for "making income balance outgo"; of the need for an "adequate but sound currency" (sharp applause for that!); promises a "good neighbor" policy in foreign affairs, but says domestic affairs must come first. Most striking of all, however, is the constant emphasis upon the need for action. Again and again comes the word " action." And after the new President has said he believes that the sort of action which is needed may be taken under the Constitution, the loudest applause of all comes for his declaration that if the occasion warrants he will not hesitate to ask for "broad executive power to wage a war against the emergency, as great as the power that would be given to me if we were in fact invaded by a foreign foe."

A ten-strike, this declaration. For the people have been sick of watching an Executive devote his strongest energies to opposing action, however questionable: they want a positive policy.

"We do not distrust the future of essential democracy," the President continues. "The people of the United States have not failed. In their need they have registered a mandate that they want direct, vigorous action. They have asked for discipline and direction under leadership. They have made me the present instrument of their wishes. In the spirit of the gift I take it."

You can turn off the radio now. You have heard what you wanted to hear. This man sounds no longer cautious, evasive. For he has seen that a tortured and bewildered people want to throw overboard the old and welcome something new; that they are sick of waiting, they want somebody who will *fight* this Depression for them and with them; they want leadership, the thrill of bold decision. And not only in his words but in the challenge of the very accents of his voice he has promised them what they want.

If only the performance measures up to the promise!

Immediate Action Follows

Action there was, in abundance; and it came fast.

On Sunday, March 5, the day after the inauguration, the new President not only called Congress to meet in special session on Thursday, but also issued a proclamation putting the bank holiday on a national basis and prohibiting the export of gold and all dealings in foreign exchange. (Thus the country went at least part way off the gold standard—on a temporary basis.)

On Thursday Congress met and passed with a whoop a law validating everything that the executive had done to date and tightening still further its control over banking operations, gold, silver, currency, and foreign exchange.

On Friday the President asked Congress for immediate action to cut Federal expenses to the bone—and Congress rushed at the task, despite the political distastefulness of slashing the veterans' allowances.

On Saturday—after a week of furious activity at the Treasury, during which regulations were devised and altered, plans for the issue of clearing-house certificates were made and abandoned, plans for the issue of new currency were promulgated, and a rough classification of banks into more and less sound was made with the aid of advice from Federal Reserve Banks and chief national bank examiners—the President announced that most of the banks of the country would open the following Monday, Tuesday, and Wednesday.

On Sunday night the President, in his first "fireside chat" [on the radio], explained to the people of the country with admirable simplicity, clarity, and persuasiveness just how the re-opening of the banks would be managed and how his hearers could help to make the process orderly.

On Monday, the 13th of March, the banks began to open. And on the same day the President asked Congress to legalize beer [modifying a law to increase allowable alcohol content]—thus closing his tremendous first ten days of office on a note of festivity.

President Roosevelt used "fireside chats" to explain his policies to the American people.

Such were the bare facts of those ten days. But the mere catalogue of them gives little idea of their overtones of significance, or of what those ten days were like to the American people.

A Potential Hornet's Nest

The predicament of the incoming Administration was staggering. A new President and new Cabinet, unaccustomed even to the ordinary routine of their positions, largely unacquainted with their staffs, and forced to rely heavily upon the services of Hoover officials who stayed on to help them, had to deal with an unprecedented emergency which confronted them with unforeseen problems. Everything had to be done at top speed. Nobody could tell what might be the future cost of mistakes made under such pressure. Nobody could be sure, for that matter, that this was not just the first of a progressive series of emergencies which would bring conditions infinitely worse. Never did a green Administration seem to be walking into such a potential hornet's nest of difficulties. . . .

An enormous majority of the population desperately wanted the New Deal to succeed. Even the Wall Street bankers were ready to give Roosevelt full powers and wish him well, wince though they might at being called money changers who had "fled from their high seats in the temple." They were badly frightened, their institutions were demoralized, their collective reputation was besmirched anyhow, their only hope lay in Roosevelt's success. The newspapers, too, were loud now with enthusiasm. For weeks they had been burying bank-panic news in the back pages; now they could let go—and out gushed, on the news pages and in the editorials, all that zest for whooping it up, for boosting, for delivering optimistic fight talks, that was innate and habitual in the American temperament. Congress, usually divided in opinion and intractable, became almost as unanimous and enthusiastic as a cheering section—because public opinion told them to. The Congressmen's mail was heavy, and the burden of it was "Support the President." It was as if a people rent by discords suddenly found themselves marching in step. . . .

Most React with Relief

Despite the fact that indirectly the bank holiday brought new distress, through new curtailments of business and new layoffs, and intensified the suffering of many people who were already hard hit, . . . the majority of Americans felt a sense of relief at having the lid of secrecy blown off. Now everything was out in the open. They felt that this trouble was temporary. They felt no shame now in being short of money—everybody seemed to be. They were all in the same boat. And they responded to one another's difficulties good-naturedly.

The grocer lent credit (what else could he do?), most hotels were glad to honor checks, shops were cordial about charge accounts. The diminished advertising columns of the newspapers contained such cheerful announcements as "IN PAYMENT FOR PASSAGE WE WILL ACCEPT CHECKS OR PROPERLY AUTHORIZED SCRIP". . . ; "RADIO CITY HAS CONFIDENCE IN AMERICA AND ITS PEOPLE—until scrip becomes available our box offices will accept checks"; "WE WILL TAKE YOUR CHECK DATED THREE MONTHS AHEAD for a three months' supply of Pepsodent for yourself and your family."

True, the shopping districts were half deserted; on the upper floors of department stores, clerks were standing about with no customers at all; there was a Saturday air about the business offices, trains were sparsely filled, stock exchanges and commodity exchanges were closed. But in the talk that buzzed everywhere there was less of foreboding than of eager and friendly excitement. . . .

A Brilliant Beginning

To this public mood President Roosevelt's first fireside chat was perfectly attuned. Quiet, uncondescending, clear, and confident, it was an incredibly skillful performance. . . . The banks opened without any such renewed panic as had been feared. They might not have done so had people realized that it was impossible, in a few days, to separate the sound banks from the unsound with any certainty, and that errors were bound to be made. The story goes that one bank had been in such bad shape that its directors decided not even to put in an application to reopen; through a clerical slip this bank was put on the wrong list, received a clean bill of health, and opened with flying colors! In some places, to be sure, there were bank runs even after the opening—runs which had to be met unquestioningly with Federal funds, lest the whole trouble begin over again. And so many banks had to be kept shut anyhow that ten per cent or more of the deposits of the country were still tied up after March 15, and the national economic machinery thus remained partially crippled. On the whole, however, the opening was an immense success. Confidence had come back with a rush; for the people had been captivated and persuaded by a President who seemed to believe in them and was giving them action, action, action.

The New Deal had made a brilliant beginning.

E V E N T **10** Congress Repeals Prohibition: December 5, 1933

A Resounding Yes Ends the Prohibition Era

by Thomas M. Coffey

The repeal of Prohibition in the United States on December 5, 1933, rubber-stamped the obvious: The nation's thirteen-year attempt to regulate the drinking habits of Americans had failed.

During Prohibition, efforts to ban the sale and manufacture of liquor proved impossible to enforce. In fact, many previously law-abiding Americans disregarded the law—at the risk of fines and prison—by purchasing moonshine liquor or by brewing it themselves. Private clubs, nightclubs, and speakeasies where illegal liquor was served grew in number, and the smuggling of illegal liquor across state borders became the norm. This, and the eventual buildup of organized crime, inflicted needless suffering on Americans at a horrendous cost in both dollars and lives. Thomas M. Coffey sums it up well: Prohibition was "a dismal blight" on the land—it was a "fiasco."

In the next article, Coffey explores the eventful day of repeal in Utah's House of Representatives, along with President Franklin D. Roosevelt's proclamation speech in response, and the nation's overall reaction to the repeal. Together there was a combined sense of jubilance, moderation, and relief. Meanwhile, the establishment of legitimate drinking facilities and the distribution of legal liquor was the next order of business. The process seemed destined for snags, but Coffey shows how the president faced the problem in a "simple

---

but practical" fashion, admonishing citizens to behave responsibly and to buy liquor from licensed dealers only, which would also take away the market from illegal bootleggers. The revenue gained from the newly levied tax on legal liquor was added incentive, and from the figures that Coffey provides detailing the actual cost of Prohibition, it was sorely needed.

Over the years, author Thomas M. Coffey has been a reporter, a movie critic, and a writer and producer for television. His books include *Agony at Easter, Imperial Tragedy*, and *Lion by the Tail* (the story of Benito Mussolini's 1935 invasion of Ethiopia).

In the assembly hall of the Utah state House of Representatives at Salt Lake City, the federal government's fourteen-year effort to banish liquor from the land came to a sudden end on the fifth of December, 1933. That afternoon at 3:32 (Mountain time), the last delegate to Utah's ratification convention—S.R. Thurman of Salt Lake City—cast a resounding "Yes" vote for the Twenty-first Amendment to the U.S. Constitution. The new amendment stated that "The eighteenth article of amendment to the Constitution of the United States is hereby repealed."

A great cheer arose from the floor and galleries as Thurman cast his vote. Everyone in the chamber realized that this made Utah the thirty-sixth state to ratify, and that the new amendment now had the three-fourths-of-all-states majority required for adoption. The convention's president, Ray L. Olson of Ogden, gaveled for silence and announced the official result. This was immediately transmitted to the White House in Washington, both by special wire and by the radio facilities of the Columbia Broadcasting Company.

Roosevelt Enjoins All to Cooperate and to Respect the Law

The proclamation President Roosevelt had written for the occasion was admonitory rather than jubilant. "I enjoin all citizens," he said, "to cooperate with the government in its endeavor to restore greater respect for law and order by confining such purchases of alcoholic beverages as they may make solely to those dealers or agents which have been duly licensed." Finally, the time had come for a serious drive against bootleggers. The government could collect its newly levied taxes on liquor only if it were purchased through "duly licensed" dealers.

Roosevelt also promised to prevent a recurrence of the "social evils" of the pre-prohibition era and asked that no state "authorize the return of the saloon either in its old form or in some modern guise." This last plea was nothing more than a political gesture. Roosevelt knew as well as everyone else that the saloon would now come back, but as a politician he was expected to deplore this fact. Even the most ardent wets had long since accepted the necessity to deplore the evils of the old saloon. The President, after paying homage to this well-established political custom, then put an end to it with the kind of simple but practical action for which he was becoming famous. Henceforth, he said, Americans must eschew the word "saloon," substituting for it the word "tavern." During these first months of his presidency, Roosevelt was such a popular figure that no one seemed to notice he was actually proclaiming the return of the saloon, if not "in its old form," then "in some modern guise."

Congress Passes the Cullen Bill

The new Democrat-dominated Congress, apparently unable to move against the depression until the new President arrived to prod it, had nevertheless moved against prohibition without any prompting two weeks before his March 4 inauguration. On February 16 the Senate had voted 63-23 to submit the Twenty-first Amendment for ratification by state conventions. Four days later, the House of Representatives had done likewise by another overwhelming vote of 289 to 121. When Roosevelt entered the Oval Office, there was only one significant repeal gesture left for him to make. On March 13 he proposed that Congress immediately modify the Volstead Act [the Prohibition Enforcement Act; defines any beverage containing 0.5 alcohol or more as "intoxicating"] to allow the sale of light wines and 3.2 percent beer. As a result, Congress passed the Cullen Bill and on April 7 much of the nation enjoyed a small beer binge in preparation for the big hard-liquor binge expected to take place the minute the Eighteenth Amendment was repealed.

Counting the Cost of Prohibition

Everyone assumed the country was ready for a celebration. A dismal blight had been lifted from the land. Despite the social and personal miseries caused by excessive drinking, liquor had proved as impossible as sin to eliminate, and the attempt at its prohibition had produced a fiasco as tragic as it was expensive.

The day this fiasco ended, the Justice Department tried to add up the cost of prohibition and discovered that the federal government alone had spent $129 million in the attempt to enforce it. Ninety-two federal agents and 178 civilians had been killed in acts of violence against each other. More than a half-million people had been convicted in federal courts for offenses against the liquor laws. In addition, millions of others had repeatedly broken these laws, thereby encouraging in themselves and the people around them a diminution of respect for all law. And billions of man-hours had been wasted in the continuous fourteen-year debate between the wets and the drys—a debate in which each side poured forth upon the other a constant deluge of misinformation, delusion, and deceit.

The Nation Celebrates

It was not surprising that President Roosevelt should welcome repeal with sober warnings. Much more surprising was the fact that the nation itself welcomed repeal with fairly sober celebrations.

Chicago, of course, was an exception. Its more than seven thousand illegal drinking establishments began filling up long before the moment of Utah's ratification. Only the big wholesalers and hotels, watched closely by federal revenue men, observed the deadline. St. Louis remained technically dry even after the deadline because the state of Missouri hadn't yet got around to canceling its enforcement law. The city's bars became crowded anyway as people left their offices after 5 P.M., but those who hoped to enjoy their first legal drinks on the way home that night had to settle once more for bootlegged drinks.

Missouri was one of twenty-eight states that still had constitutional or statutory prohibition, although most of them were in the process of annulling it. Nevada was not among them. Nevadans were so well prepared for repeal that within ten minutes of Utah's ratification, liquor stores throughout the state were selling well-known brands across the counters. Some of the state's speakeasies, long since as wide open as its brothels and gambling casinos, didn't even stop serving long enough to observe the moment when they were declared legal. It was simply business as usual.

There was no celebration in Los Angeles or Hollywood. While

numerous nightclubs were open, most of the movie stars stayed at home, perhaps to avoid the crowds which were anticipated but did not materialize.

In Detroit, Henry Ford offended the drys and startled everyone else by serving bottled beer at a public luncheon in honor of his new 1934 V-8 model. In most Eastern cities, where the time was already 5:32 P.M. when Utah ratified, it was too late for all but a few wholesalers to supply the newly licensed retailers. Philadelphia, as a result, was even more quiet than usual the night prohibition ended. Boston, where prohibition had never been honored very seriously, treated this night like any other one.

In New York, Pauline Sabin said hopefully, "I am confident that whatever celebrations usher in the return of legal liquor, they will be short-lived, and that once the custom of drinking is no longer shrouded in secrecy we shall settle down to temperance and moderation."

Meanwhile, the city's entire police force of 19,000 men was mobilized to handle the throngs expected in the streets. Surprisingly, only the Times Square area filled with people, and even there the crowd was well behaved. Arrests did not exceed the daily average for the previous five years. Perhaps this was because many would-be celebrants had trouble finding drinks. The police, after fourteen years of tolerating speakeasies, had suddenly begun raiding all those which hadn't procured licenses. Since licenses had been issued to only three thousand establishments in the metropolitan area, repeal brought an immediate drop of several thousand in the number of drinking places. And few of the three thousand licensed places had been able to procure liquor between the time it became legal and the time the warehouses closed. The city's two largest warehouses had closed even before Utah ratified. From those which stayed open later, only fifty-four truckloads of bonded whisky had been released.

Consequently, liquor was so scarce that some New Yorkers longed for the return of prohibition so they could buy a drink. Only those fortunate enough to find tables at the large hotels or ex-speakeasies such as the Stork Club, the Embassy, and Twenty-One, which had been transformed into supper clubs, could be assured of as much liquor as they wished. In order to be served, customers had to be seated at tables, because New York had passed a law (soon to be revoked) forbidding the sale of drinks at a bar.

A Former Governor's Reaction to the Repeal

Late in the afternoon of December 5, an enterprising newsman, finding almost nothing to report about repeal on the streets of New York, decided to interview former Governor Al Smith.

Having been the first significant national political figure to declare himself wet, and having fought against prohibition since the moment it began, Smith could be said to have sacrificed his career to the wet cause. As a result he now suffered great bitterness—a bitterness compounded by the fact that his protegé, Franklin D. Roosevelt, was reaping the benefits of the spadework Smith had done [Smith lost his bid for the presidency in 1928], and at the same time was imposing on the country a socioeconomic program which Smith considered unsound.

Today, however, there was no apparent bitterness in Al Smith. When the reporter and his photographer entered the paneled office he now occupied as president of the Empire State Building Corporation, the former governor came forward to greet them with his famous beaming smile. He had just received the news of Utah's ratification and he was delighted.

In honor of the occasion, the reporter asked, would Smith be willing to pose for a picture with a drink in his hand?

Smith declined with a laugh. "I never drink," he said, "in the daytime."

E V E N T **10** **Congress Repeals Prohibition: December 5, 1933**

Prohibition's Repeal Has Mixed Economic Results

by *Newsweek*

With the government's newly levied tax on liquor firmly in place and the licensing of drinking establishments a stiff requirement, the repeal of Prohibition on December 5, 1933, was seen by some Americans as a golden opportunity to profit from liquor legally. Winegrowers, distillers, brewers, and others approached the following year with high hopes, and with the nation still in the grips of depression, any degree of optimism could be viewed as a miracle.

But according to *Newsweek* in the following article published one year later, the impact of the repeal was disappointing. Assessing the difficulties of that year, *Newsweek* retells the confusion, the complaints, and the joys that some experienced. Liquor stores and hotels, for example, were upset over the income they had lost to smaller competitors who had successfully whittled away some of their profits. Apparently, even department stores were selling drinks.

Others reacted in a mixed fashion according to *Newsweek*. Winegrowers were unhappy, but brewers were elated. Some longed for Prohibition again, when liquor was cheaper, but others thought the world was a better place. But the most disappointed of all it would seem were those in the Alcohol Control Administration, who had discovered early on that bootleggers were well entrenched in illegal

---

"REPEAL: A Year Ends; Liquor Men Confused; Wine Growers Sad; Brewers Happy; Taxes Disappointing; Bootleggers Plentiful," *Newsweek*, vol. 4, December 8, 1934, pp. 3–4.

operations and were making good profits. One legacy of Prohibition had been the increased consumption of hard liquor in America, which bootleggers anticipated all too well.

With a spot of rye, a Martini, a bottle of beer—or a glass of water—citizens toasted the end of repeal's first year on Wednesday. Some complained the rye was harsher than the bootleg they drank in dry years. Others grumbled that the gin in Martinis cost too much. One group longed for a return of prohibition. Another group felt repeal had made the world a better place.

Liquor merchants also disagreed on the merits of legal liquor. Hotel men, ringing up 35 cents on the cash register for each cocktail sold, were thankful for the new source of revenue.

Yet experience has modified their last year's optimism.

Confusion: Hotels have had to fight unforeseen competitors. A few years ago Childs restaurants emphasized vitamins and calories and went in for ascetic vegetarianism. Today they advertise cocktails and wine. Tea rooms and "Coffee Pots" reach out for their share of liquor profits.

Liquor stores, catering to the package trade, made the same complaint. One out of every four stores that joined last year's rush to get in on a "good thing" has closed its doors. Yet the field is still overcrowded. Bargain beer at chain stores, 50-cent sherry crowding low-priced chintzes on department store bargain counters, and special-priced gin featured with two-pants suits in clothing stores, kept the small liquor dealer hustling.

Many distillers, wholesalers, and importers have also been disillusioned. Business has fallen far short of expectations. This group blames high taxes, which raise prices, cut sales, and encourage heavy competition from tax-evading bootleggers. At the same time, price wars cut into profits. In the beginning, confusing regulations increased both expenses and worry. Several States required that their tax stamps be pasted over bottle tops with nothing covering them, conflicting with a similar requirement for tax stamps of the Federal Government. Minnesota's demand for a guarantee of purity on bottle labels was counter to the Federal ban on the use of the word "pure" on whisky labels.

Of all those who hoped to make their fortunes in a wet country, wine-makers and grape-growers, centering in California, wear the longest faces. They knew that hard liquor had grown in popularity under prohibition. But they hoped and planned for at least as much wine drinking as had prevailed before the war. This estimate, they have sadly discovered, was 40 per cent too high.

This Fall many vineyardists in California's $350,000,000 industry let the crop rot on the vines. Native vintners have to fight against imported wines reputedly superior to domestic. Home-made wine is another stumbling block.

Joy: With a half-year start on the hard-liquor business, brewers wound up their first year of legal operation last June. They found themselves in clover. Instead of the predicted 30,000,000 barrels, they had sold 38,000,000. In the subsequent five months they maintained about the same average increase.

The new liquor business proved a blessing to advertising firms. Outlays for publicity of some liquor concerns ran to almost $2,000,000 a year. Newspapers, magazines, and radio stations gleaned a substantial revenue. Glassmakers have also had a good year. The rush to stock up the pantry with the dozen different shapes and sizes of glasses needed for genteel, non-speakeasy drinking brought them their best year since the boom.

Government: Optimists a year ago predicted that Federal tax receipts on liquor would reach $1,000,000,000. Even conservatives, who expected half that sum, were over-sanguine. In the first year of repeal, $400,000,000 flowed into the Federal Treasury. State treasuries collected their quotas, topped by New York's $35,000,000.

Joseph H. Choate Jr., lanky head of the Federal Alcohol Control Administration, realized soon after he took office that the bootlegger had no intention of going out of business. Mr. Choate believes lawbreakers have marketed 50,000,000 gallons of hard liquor—more than has been sold by licensed manufacturers. To staunch the illicit flow Mr. Choate and Secretary of the Treasury Henry Morgenthau organized a corps of 1,400 agents. In eleven months they seized 10,947 stills.

Some bootleg is peddled direct to licensed dealers, who pour it into empty trade-marked bottles and sell it over the counter. Bootleggers also counterfeit the packages of legitimate, advertised brands, complete with bogus labels and revenue stamps.

Secretary Morgenthau believes his agents can eventually stop bootlegging. But Mr. Choate is skeptical. Agents, he thinks, will never win the battle unaided. Before the next Congress he will plead for lower taxes as a means of reducing the bootlegger's margin of profit. Secretary Morgenthau, guardian of the purse-strings, promises to oppose any such change.

John Barleycorn: F. Scott McBride, aggressive ex-clergyman who heads the Anti-Saloon League, considers repeal "the most complete failure" in the history of efforts to solve the liquor problem.

"Thousands of women, girls, and boys," he says, "have become the victims of drink. . . . Murders, suicides, and crimes of all kinds caused by intoxication are reported daily."

• Under repeal some States have raised old bogies. Illinois passed a law permitting "taverns" and giving control of the licenses to local authorities. This caused a rebirth of the alliance between politicians and saloonkeepers. Popular disgust showed itself in last month's election. Citizens in 600 Illinois precincts voted to banish the "taverns" by local option.

• In Coatesville, a small city west of Philadelphia, arrests for drunkenness under repeal jumped 1,100 per cent from the last pre-repeal year. Lesser increases occurred in most parts of the country. Apologists said policemen arrest many wobbling figures they would have ignored during prohibition.

• College students behave better under repeal, according to their own testimony. Hip-flasks at proms have passed out of favor. Some college officials doubt their pupils' sobriety. Dennis Enright, caretaker at the Harvard Stadium, gathered up 1,546 empty liquor bottles after this year's football game with Army.

• Disappointed local producers got some solace from reports from abroad. French vines this year bent earthward under a bumper crop of large, luscious grapes. Wine sold for as low as 8 cents a quart. The supply of barrels was not great enough to store the crop. Thrifty French growers allowed vineyard workers to drink their fill. Press dispatches reported that men, mules, and donkeys in the Roussillon and cognac districts could hardly walk straight on the roads.

• New York City health reports indicate that repeal has added to the span of life. In legal liquor's first year, deaths from alcoholism in the city dropped to 533, the lowest in ten years. The all-time high for alcoholic deaths was 942 in 1931.

• In Mount Sherman, Arkansas, beer barrel manufacturers last week made James T. Richmond a generous offer for part of the timber on his 160-acre property. Indignantly he replied: "I've fought the use of intoxicating liquor for years and I'm certainly not going to change my doctrine by selling timber to make beer barrels."

His decision stood, he said, despite the fact that the drought wiped out his crop, wolves killed his milk goats, cholera took all his hogs, and his mother died.

E V E N T **11** **Picasso's *Guernica* Debuts at the International Exhibition in Paris: July 1937**

War and Art: Picasso's *Guernica* Debuts in Paris

by Roland Penrose

By 1937 Pablo Picasso (1881–1973) was well established in the art world, having painted his first major work, *The Picador*, in 1890. He was particularly known for his development of cubism (1907), a modern art form that uses geometric shapes and lines to define subject matters. According to author Roland Penrose, the public at the time often viewed cubism as "abstract or even demented" art.

A strong opponent of Spanish dictator Francisco Franco, Picasso was in anguish over the Spanish republic's loss to the fascist Franco regime. Aided by fascist Germany and Italy, Franco had been bombing Spanish civilians. Picasso was commissioned by the Spanish Republicans to paint a mural expressing their outrage; the mural would then be displayed at the upcoming International Exhibition in Paris. After the Germans bombed a small Basque town called Guernica, killing sixteen hundred of its seven thousand inhabitants and destroying 70 percent of the town, Picasso painted a mural based on the tragic event.

The black-and-white mural took Picasso less than two months to paint. Public reaction to *Guernica* was mixed, although wide acclaim would follow over time. Beyond *Guernica*'s immediate im-

---

Roland Penrose, *Picasso: His Life and Work*. Berkeley: University of California Press, 1981.

pact as a protest against war, Penrose sheds further light on the mythic symbolism of the mural. Of particular note, according to Penrose, is the universality of *Guernica* in its application to future catastrophic events or acts of terror. Penrose calls it a timeless image that captures the emotions of humanity for all time.

Because of Franco's continued rule in Spain, Picasso refused to allow *Guernica* to be shown in Spain. It was not until 1981, after Picasso's death and the reestablishment of a democratic government in Spain, that Picasso's lawyers finally allowed *Guernica* to be housed in an art gallery in Spain. Picasso is considered one of the most famous painters of the twentieth century, and one of the most influential. His astonishing output included thousands of paintings, prints, sculptures, and ceramics.

Artist, curator, and author Roland Penrose was the founder of the Institute of Contemporary Art in London. A member of the surrealist group during the 1920s, he was a close friend of Pablo Picasso and other artists. He organized many major expositions throughout his career for the Tate Gallery, New York's Museum of Modern Art, and the New York Cultural Center. He wrote numerous books on art and artists, and in 1966 he was knighted for his services to the arts.

At Le Tremblay [France] Picasso was happily detached from the disquieting preoccupations of Paris. His short visits gave him the opportunity to enjoy a replica of family life; but on returning to Paris he again became involved in the growing anxieties of his friends. The news from Spain was bad, and as in all civil wars, where even brothers can be divided against each other, the situation was vexed by mixed loyalties, suspicion and hate. His mother in Barcelona sent news of the burning of a convent within a few yards of the apartment in which she lived with her widowed daughter and five grandchildren. For weeks the rooms had reeked with the stench, and her keen black eyes, the model for her son's, ran with tears from the smoke.

To the group of young poets, painters and architects who had recently organized the exhibitions of his work, the defence of democratic liberty had become a matter of life and death. Many had hastily taken up arms and departed for the front. Others, disproving fascist propaganda, which claimed that the art treasures of Spain were being pillaged and burnt by unruly mobs of anarchists, set to work on surveys of neglected ancient monuments and the organization of new museums. In Paris also there was a remarkable unity among intellectuals in support of Republican Spain. . . .

Picasso Is Commissioned to Paint a Mural

It was this year [1937] that had been chosen by the French Government for a great International Exhibition, and it was of great importance to the Spanish Republicans that their Government should be well represented [at the Spanish Pavilion]. . . . Picasso had already consented to produce some manifestation which would make his sympathies clear to the world, and there was much speculation as to what form it would take. . . .

The spring passed, however, without any sign that Picasso had discovered what form his contribution to the Spanish Pavilion should take. The problems that arose were complex and their solution greatly intrigued those who looked to him for a valid expression of the feelings of millions of people outraged by the civil war. Since the painting was to be used as the main feature in one of the pavilions in an international exhibition which would be visited by people from all over the world, it was hoped that its appeal would be couched in a style which would deeply affect the masses. Was it possible that the inventor of Cubism and strange distortions, styles which the public in general considered abstract or even demented, could make an appeal to ordinary people? The Spanish Government had asked Picasso to take on this task, knowing that his reputation was in itself an attraction. . . . As usual Picasso decided to tackle the problem in his own way. Trusting his inspiration, when the time came he painted a picture whose strength could be ignored by no one. Its impact on the thousands of visitors to the exhibition came as a shock even to those who could not fathom its meaning. But as later the public grew slowly more familiar with its idiom, it came to be recognized as a lasting protest against war, surpassing the limitations of partisan propaganda and remaining valid even after the cause for which it had been painted had met with defeat. . . .

Picasso Finds His Theme

On 29 April 1937 news reached Paris that German bombers in Franco's pay had wiped out the small market town of Guernica, the ancient capital of the Basques. [General Francisco Franco led the fascist movement in Spain.] This gratuitous outrage, perpetrated at an hour when the streets were thronged with people, roused Picasso from melancholy to anger. Acting as a catalyst to the anxiety and indignation mingled within him, it gave him the theme he had been seeking. . . .

The first characters to appear on his stage in hasty sketches were the horse, the bull, and a woman stretching out from a window with a lamp in her hand to throw light on the calamity in which they were all suddenly involved. In successive versions, some drawn rapidly in pencil, numbered and dated, and others painted on canvas, the personalities of the actors began to evolve, while at the same time they appeared together in compositions. From the beginning Picasso chose the stricken horse as a central feature.

The *Guernica* Mural Grows

Ten days after the first sketch, a canvas eleven and a half feet high and nearly twenty-six feet long had been set up at one end of the room in the rue des Grands Augustins. It was stretched from wall to wall, and from the tiled floor below to the massive oak beams supporting the rafters. The room, though it seemed vast, was not quite high enough for the width of the canvas, and it could only be fitted in by sloping it backwards, which meant that the upper part had to be reached with a long brush from the top of a ladder. In spite of having often to climb to this perilous position Picasso worked fast, and the outline of the first version was sketched in almost as soon as the canvas was up. . . .

As the painting developed it was possible to watch the balance that Picasso kept between the misery caused by war, seen in the anguish of the women, the pain of the wounded horse or the pitiful remains of the dead warrior; and the defiant hope of an ultimate victory. Many writers have tried to interpret Picasso's symbolism and often they have committed the error of oversimplification. Juan Larrea, in an extensive and otherwise authoritative study of *Guernica*, states surprisingly that the horse transfixed with a pike represents Nationalist (Franco) Spain. To others the horse and its rider are the heroic victims of a brutal attack from the bull; but on examination we find, particularly in the early versions, nothing to suggest that the bull is in this case the villain. On the contrary he appears to be searching the horizon for the enemy, who is in fact not present in the scene at all. His enemy is the common enemy of all mankind, too vile and too universal to be contained in a single image. What we see in the painting is the effect of his enormity: the dead child, the house in flames, lacerated bodies, hysterical cries of agony and looks of astonishment that such things are possible. . . .

The Simplicity of *Guernica*

It is the simplicity of *Guernica* that makes it a picture which can be readily understood. The forms are divested of all complications which would distract from their meaning. The flames that rise from the burning house and flicker on the dress of the falling woman are described by signs as unmistakable as those used by primitive artists. The nail-studded hoof, the hand with deeply furrowed palm, and the sun illuminated with an electric light bulb, are drawn with a child-like simplicity, startling in its directness. . . .

Public Reaction to *Guernica*

Before two months from the day Picasso made his first sketch had elapsed, the great canvas *Guernica* was ready to take its place in the Spanish Pavilion at the Paris Exhibition. Economies enforced by the war had required their plans to be modest, but the architects had reserved a place of honour for it, and near by they set up two of the large statues made four years earlier at Boisgeloup. In the courtyard in front was a mercury fountain designed by Alexander Calder, and Joan Miró also contributed a mural which was placed at the head of a stairway leading to a gallery above.

The immediate reactions of the public were confused, and the press was divided on political grounds. The less numerous critics of the right wing had no hesitation in condemning it for its intention as well as its appearance, while the left wing supported it, though the less enlightened among them would have preferred a painting which was an obvious call to arms. Others with an equally grave misconception of the poetic nature of the painting hailed it as a form of social art or 'social realism' with a predominant political purpose. Those who appreciated its true nature at once were the intellectuals from many countries, who recognized in it a great work of art and a crystallization of their feelings about the horrors of war and Fascism, which for them had become almost synonymous.

Praise from the Art World

Zervos produced a number of the *Cahiers d'Art* almost entirely devoted to the painting, and including Dora Maar's admirable photos of its progress, as well as the preliminary studies and small canvases. It contained articles by Zervos himself, Jean Cassou, Georges Duthuit, Pierre Mabille, Michel Leiris, a poem by Paul Eluard and an important contribution by the Spanish Catholic poet José Bergamin. Throughout, their praise for Picasso, who had put on record with such majesty the calamity of Guernica, is tempered with a sense of foreboding. 'In a rectangle black and white such as that in which ancient tragedy appeared to us, Picasso sends us our announcement of our mourning: all that we love is going to die, and that is why it was necessary to this degree that all that we love should embody itself, like the effusions of a last farewell, in something unforgettably beautiful.' These words of Michel Leiris reveal the gratitude felt towards Picasso for expressing the despair of those who knew themselves and their hopes to be menaced, realizing that they were incapable of extricating society from its approaching doom. He had interpreted their forebodings and so made their anxiety more bearable.

A Universal Meaning

Guernica has been compared with other great works such as *The Massacre at Chios* by Delacroix, Géricault's *Raft of the Medusa* and Goya's *Madrid 2 May*. In the scale of its monumental appeal it has much in common with these paintings, but whereas they all used the recognized idiom of their time to portray catastrophes that had occurred, in *Guernica* Picasso found a more universal means of conveying the emotion centred round a given event, and in consequence arrived at a timeless and transcendental image. In addition, the symbolic use of the familiar and humble enabled him to present disaster in an emotional way without overstatement. It is not the horror of an actual occurrence with which we are presented; it is a universal tragedy made vivid to us by the myth he has reinvented and the revolutionary directness with which it is presented. The power of *Guernica* will grow.

EVENT 12 "The War of the Worlds" Airs on Radio: October 30, 1938

Thousands Mistake "The War of the Worlds" for a Martian Invasion

by *Newsweek*

British novelist H.G. Wells first published his famous tale of Martian invasion, *The War of the Worlds*, in 1898, but it was its later revival as a CBS radio dramatization in 1938 by actor Orson Welles that would forever place it in the archives of U.S. radio history. The scheduled CBS airing was for October 30, Halloween Eve, on Orson Welles's *Mercury Theater of the Air* program. According to the following article, originally published in *Newsweek* magazine, CBS officials had suspected the story might "bore" audiences. In order to "pep up the story," they decided to change its locale from Great Britain to the state of New Jersey. The effect was astounding. Thousands of listeners mistook the fictional piece for a real eyewitness account of an invasion from outer space and panicked.

Newsweek surmises that one of the reasons people had misinterpreted Welles's narration was due to their absence at the beginning of the program. Apparently, most listeners had been tuned in to a rival station's broadcast of the popular Charlie McCarthy show. When that show ended twenty minutes later, the "dial twirlers," as *Newsweek* called them, twirled their radio dials to "The War of the Worlds," but having missed the opening announcement that the

"Dialed Hysteria," *Newsweek*, November 7, 1938, p. 13.

story was fictitious, they could only draw one conclusion: The invasion was real.

Of course, much of the hysteria generated was due to the wild imaginations of those spreading the news. *Newsweek* reports that one person claimed to have heard the "swish" of Martian invaders and another that they could actually view the battle through binoculars. For critics of radio, however, the event simply confirmed their argued assessment that radio was a dangerous tool capable of manipulating mass audiences.

Last Sunday night, between 8 P.M. and 9 P.M. (E.S.T.), thousands of radio listeners were shocked silly when they tuned in a CBS program and heard a voice shout in breathless news-broadcast style "Flash! Meteor reported landing near Grovers Mill, N.J. . . . 1,500 killed . . . no, it's not a meteor . . . it's a flying metallic cylinder . . . gas sweeping New Jersey . . . invaders flying over the nation, raining bombs . . . death rays . . ."

Actually, CBS was resuming a series of dramatic programs prepared by Orson Welles, boy wonder of the theatre. Some radio executives had supposed that a dramatization of H.G. Wells' 40-year-old fantasy "The War of the Worlds" would bore listeners. So to pep up the story of Martian monsters who terrorized Great Britain, the locale was changed to this country, with Martians laying waste to the New Jersey countryside.

But the radio chain had not counted on the reaction of countless thousands who had spent the first twenty minutes of the hour tuned in on a rival NBC attraction, Charlie McCarthy, ventriloquists's dummy and fans' favorite. When Charlie had finished his brief stint, these listeners joined other dial twirlers and missed an initial announcement that identified the program's fictitious nature; likewise, they missed or ignored three similar subsequent warnings. On all these, already made danger-conscious by the recent war scare the effect of Wells-Welles realism was galvanic.

As though an emotional electric switch had been turned on, a wave of mass hysteria broke over the entire country. Police stations, hospitals, and newspaper offices were flooded with phone calls from fear-frozen citizens asking how they could escape destruction and how to get gas masks. In a score of states, weeping, hysterical men and women prayed for deliverance. Hundreds fainted. Doctors and nurses volunteered assistance.

As rumors spread, imaginations went wild: one citizen reported he had heard the "swish" of the Martian visitors, another heard machine-gun fire, and a man with binoculars atop a Manhattan building "saw" the flames of battle. In Brooklyn a man phoned the police station: "We can hear the firing all the way here, and I want a gas mask. I'm a taxpayer."

In front of a Newark, N.J., apartment house, police found twenty families had started to remove their furniture—and their faces were swathed in wet towels to repel poisonous gas. A Pittsburgh husband found his wife with a bottle of poison, screaming: "I'd rather die this way than that." And at Princeton University, Dr. Arthur F. Buddington, chairman of the Geology Department, gathered his field equipment and set out to get a specimen of the "meteor."

Significance

Those who argue that radio is the strongest arm of dictators, since it reduces an entire country to the size of one room, gasped at the graphic example of its power over susceptible multitudes. Never had radio's ability to control people been so vividly proved, nor provoked so much widespread indignation.

Within the industry, the incident brought fear of increased censorship from Washington, as Sen. Clyde Herring of Iowa came out for legislation to curb such "Hallowe'en bogymen." While the FCC [Federal Communications Commission] withheld action Monday pending further study, radio executives privately forecast conferences to bring about more caution in presentation of material.

EVENT 12 "The War of the Worlds" Airs on Radio: October 30, 1938

Martian Hysteria Invades the Radio Industry

by Robert J. Brown

The following article, excerpted from *Manipulating the Ether: The Power of Broadcast Radio in Thirties America* (1998), author Robert J. Brown details the repercussions that rocked the radio industry following actor Orson Welles's broadcast of "The War of the Worlds" on CBS in 1938. Overnight, the issue of censorship, suddenly fueled by the Martian hysteria that had duped Americans into false belief the night before, loomed bigger than ever. The Federal Communications Commission (FCC) announced an immediate investigation of CBS's conduct. In addition to the FCC's quick response, politicians, radio commentators, and journalists were debating the latest uproar. CBS seemed destined for trouble.

That same day CBS went on air with a public statement of apology, but it was only the beginning according to Brown. All four networks had developed a "profound sense of responsibility" in making sure a similar broadcast error never happened again. Together they agreed to work on a method of self-regulation. In the end, several policy changes were developed and put into effect. For example, the use of words like *flash* or *bulletin* during fictional programs would now be restricted to prevent audiences from mistakenly believing they were listening to a live news report. The general goal was to make sure a distinct difference existed between what was real and what was not. Because of the networks' decision to self-

---

Robert J. Brown, *Manipulating the Ether: The Power of Broadcast Radio in Thirties America*. Jefferson, NC: McFarland & Company, Inc., 1998.

regulate, the FCC decided that government intervention would no longer be necessary.

Brown's essay brings to light the lessons learned from the broadcast, in particular, the increased awareness of radio's powerful hold over audiences. One radio commentator suggested that if the public could be so easily tricked into believing in a Martian invasion, could they not also be "frightened into fanaticism," as in the fear of communism, or "terrorized into subservience to leadership" because of some "imaginable menace," such as that experienced under dictators such as Adolf Hitler, Benito Mussolini, or Joseph Stalin?

A surprising effect of Welles's broadcast was radio's loss of credibility with its listeners. Brown points to the nation's reaction to the attack on Pearl Harbor in 1941 as an example. Apparently, many people responded to the reports with disbelief, suspecting yet another trick. Perhaps more surprising is that "The War of the Worlds" continues to dupe and frighten people years later. Similar reenactments in other countries as well as in the United States have caused mixed reactions over the years. Even as recent as 1994, when a modern television version of "The War of the Worlds" was aired again on Halloween Eve, the response—though not near that of 1938—caused fearful listeners to flood police and radio stations across the United States with calls.

Robert J. Brown is pursuing a Ph.D. in history at Syracuse University, New York.

On the heels of the tumult generated by the broadcast [of "The War of the Worlds" in 1938], the radio industry braced itself for the inevitably harsh government reaction. On October 31, Federal Communications Commission [FCC] officials indicated that they intended to review the script and conduct an inquiry to determine whether "public interest warranted official action." FCC chairman Frank McNinch ordered an immediate investigation into CBS's conduct. In the process, he set off a heated debate between those who had been continually advocating censorship of radio and those who staunchly opposed it.

Because of radio's enormous influence and expansive reach, the United States government had always been "vitally concerned with the proper control and direction of this mighty medium of communication." While the 1934 Federal Communications Act denied the FCC the power of direct censorship, it called upon that body to ensure that the public interest was in no manner threatened by radio programming. In the minds of many government officials, "this included programs that were meant to terrorize the population."

During the New Deal, "there had been a movement, coincident with the increasing centralization of authority in Washington, for stronger control and firmer regulation of radio." Proponents of this scheme sought "to make the medium more an organ of government, if not a direct arm," as in many states of Europe. Radio in the United States was government-licensed but not government-owned. In contrast to the continental system, "censorship was infrequent and federal agencies like the FCC had laid down few rules with which to govern the medium." As a result, "broadcast officials were expected to maintain this traditional liberty by acting responsibly." Individual stations and networks were given the freedom to choose their own programs and fashion their own codes of conduct, but they were expected to be self-regulating. If the FCC determined that a station or network's policies were not in harmony with the public interest, "its broadcasting license could fail to achieve renewal, or could be revoked.". . .

When the [Orson] Welles program [*Mercury Theater of the Air*] sparked a nationwide panic, industry observers "felt that radio had gone too far, and that nothing could prevent immediate government retaliation." Upon initiating hearings, Frank McNinch declared the broadcast "regrettable" and remarked, "The widespread public reaction . . . is another demonstration of the power and force of radio, and points out again the serious public responsibility of those who are licensed to operate stations." Radio commentator Hugh Johnson observed that "the witch-burning Mr. McNinch" now had "a new excuse to extend the creeping hand of government restrictions of free speech by way of radio censorship." George Henry Payne, who had spearheaded a campaign against the use of horror in children's programming, "rebuked the industry for its bad taste." Commissioner Paul A. Walker "resolved himself to be stern in this case," and Senator Clyde Herring of Iowa stated his intention to introduce a bill for "controlling such abuses as were heard over the radio" that night. Herring's legislation proposed the establishment of a censorship board "to which all radio scripts would have to be submitted prior to broadcast."

There were also many voices that denounced any kind of government action. Commissioner T.A.M. Craven remarked:

> I feel that the Commission should proceed with the utmost caution to avoid the danger of censoring what shall or shall not be broadcast over the radio. I also feel that in this case caution should be exercised so that any FCC action will not tend to handicap the development of the dramatic arts in broadcasting.

Many opponents of censorship believed that the broadcast had been nothing more than a "first-class bedtime story" and that the newspapers were responsible for making "nationwide turmoil out of a tempest in a teapot." Surprisingly, some newspapers came out in support of their electronic rival. The editor of the New York *World Telegram* stated:

> Of course it should never happen again. But we don't agree with those who are arguing that the Sunday night broadcast showed a need for strict government censorship of radio programs. . . . Better to have American radio remain free to make occasional blunders than start on a course that might, in time, deprive it of the freedom to broadcast the uncensored truth.

. . . In numerous surveys, it was clear that those opposing censorship represented the majority. When asked, "Which do you think would be better for people in this country—if radio were run by the government or by private business?" over 73 percent opted for private ownership. . . .

CBS Responds

The full force of any government retaliation was sure to descend on CBS. As a result, the network, which had previously given Welles free rein, was incensed, and [CBS head William] Paley was under considerable pressure to discipline the young prodigy. When reporters and policemen darted into the studio after the broadcast, network officials drove the entire Mercury cast into a back office. While this was going on, CBS staff commandeered every script and recording of the program and "locked them up or had them destroyed." To keep them away from public view, the Mercury Players were detained until the early morning hours. Rumors that Welles and his company would be "expelled from the network" abounded. The next day, the only souls to be seen at network headquarters were "sound mixers and elevator men."

The public reaction to the program was so distressing to CBS executives that they refused any references to it over the air. This was the tacit policy of the industry as a whole. When Fred Allen intended to "lampoon the gullible public" in a comedic skit, NBC officials adamantly refused. On October 31, CBS released an official statement of apology to its full network:

> The Columbia Broadcasting System regrets that some listeners to the Orson Welles *Mercury Theater on the Air* program last night mistook fantasy for fact. . . . Naturally it was neither Columbia's nor the Mercury Theater's intention to mislead anyone . . . and when it became evident that a part of the audience had been disturbed by the performance, five announcements were read over the network later in the evening to reassure those listeners.

Broadcasting Policies Change

The Welles broadcast and its aftershocks inspired in all four networks a profound "sense of responsibility in seeing to it that such a situation [did] not occur again." Many industry executives came to agree with the *New York Times* when it opined:

> The trouble is inherent in the method of radio broadcasting as manifested at present in this country. It can only be cured by a deeply searching self-regulation in which every element of the radio industry should join. Radio is new but it has adult responsibilities. It has not mastered the materials it uses. It does many things which the newspapers learned long ago not to do, such as mixing its news with advertising. Newspapers know the two must be rigidly separated and plainly marked. The "War of the Worlds's" bloodcurdling fiction was offered in exactly the manner that real news was given and interwoven with convincing actualities.

After careful consideration of its policy, CBS decided to redefine its role as both purveyor of news and provider of entertainment. To ensure that the two functions would remain distinct (and would never be allowed to dangerously and imperceptibly blend), the network issued an official statement on November 1: "The Program Department hereafter will not use the technique of a simulated news broadcast within a dramatization when the circumstances of the broadcast could cause immediate alarm to

Orson Welles rehearses a radio program for CBS. Welles's "War of the Worlds" broadcast caused panic among listeners.

numbers of listeners." In order to keep "what is fiction from striking the listener's ear as news," NBC, CBS and MBS all agreed that such terms as "flash" and "bulletin" would be used only with the utmost discretion and only in situations of transcendent importance. Recognizing that the "human voice was a powerful instrument," radio announcers would henceforth endeavor to "handle news without the slightest color or melodrama." It was suggested that fictional treatments of real-life situations and all dramatizations of controversial subjects that featured impersonations of prominent personages be strictly banned. As a result, the *March of Time* had to change its format from "re-enactments to on-the-spot reports by remote broadcast."

Since the Welles program demonstrated that tuning in late could lead to misinterpretation, it became necessary for announcers to reiterate the nature of their programs: "For those of you who have tuned in late . . ." Live broadcasts and recordings had to be clearly distinguished by labels such as "This is coming to you live," "The following is transcribed," "By transcription," or "Portions of the preceding have been transcribed." In addition, the networks were careful that all warlike sound effects, particularly bomb explosions and rifle fire, were clearly distinguishable from their real-life counterparts. Thus, the trademark opening of the popular crime drama *Gangbusters*, which "had featured a number of martial sounds, whistles, and machine gun chatter," had to be altered. . . .

These changes significantly increased in importance when the Second World War began. . . . The networks joined in September 1939 to issue a combined "Memorandum of European War Coverage":

> [The networks will make] every effort consistent with the news itself to keep out of their broadcasts horror, suspense, and undue excitement. . . . Broadcasters will at all times, try to distinguish between official news obtained from responsible official or unofficial sources. . . .

The efforts of CBS and the other networks had the desired effect: They prevented government intervention. On November 7, 1938, National Association of Broadcasters president Neville Miller declared:

> The Columbia Broadcasting System has taken steps to insure that such program techniques will never be used again. This instance emphasizes the responsibility we assume in the use of radio and renews our determination to fulfill to the highest degree our obligation to the public.

The next day, the FCC announced that no reprisals would be initiated against CBS. . . .

A New Awareness of Radio's Power to Manipulate

For many observers, the Welles broadcast provided no dearth of valuable lessons for the future. To some, *War of the Worlds* was a prime example of how broadcasting could encourage "that intellectual passiveness that had already taken root among the masses which induces [them] to accept ready-made opinions as they would gospel truths." Because it "appealed only to the sense of hearing, radio could encourage listeners to relapse into a state of purely receptive activity" and could "instill dangerous ideas in the popular psyche through constant repetition." Ever since the media blitz that helped propel [Adolf] Hitler into power, Europe's intelligentsia had been warning Americans of radio's ability to manipulate the "unstable, incredulous, and irrational masses." The Welles broadcast was yet another clear demonstration of the "appalling dangers and enormous effectiveness of popular and theatrical demagoguery." In the hands of manipulative firebrands, radio constituted one of the "most dangerous weapons ever invented.". . .

[Radio commentator] Dorothy Thompson agreed:

> The greatest organizers of mass hysterias and mass delusions today are states using the radio to excite terrors, incite hatreds, inflame masses, win mass support for policies, create idolatries, abolish reason and maintain themselves in power.

The Martian program proved beyond doubt that "by clever manipulation, people can be made to swallow poison—if administered in small doses, carefully timed, and with the label of an accepted authority." The "immediate moral," Thompson asserted, "is that no political body must ever, under any circumstances, obtain a monopoly of radio."

She also observed:

> If people can be frightened out of their wits by mythical men from Mars, they can be frightened into fanaticism by the fear of the Reds, or aroused to revenge against any minority or terrorized into subservience to leadership because of any imaginable menace. . . . Welles has made a greater contribution to an understanding of Hitlerism, Mussolinism, Stalinism, anti-Semitism, and all the other terrorism of our times, more than will all the words about them that have been written.

Evidently that understanding had an effect on network executives. The aftermath of the Welles broadcast caused NBC, CBS and MBS to radically reconsider their policy of selling airtime to Father Coughlin, the Communist Party, the German-American Bund, and other proponents of political views that seemed too far out of the mainstream.

Also paying attention to the effects of the Welles broadcast was Franklin Roosevelt. The president had observed the chaos that resulted when someone counterfeited his voice during the broadcast. He was not the only one to recognize the power of the impersonation, and the number of requests from advertisers and dramatists for permission to imitate the chief executive's voice on the air increased markedly. Not wanting to relinquish his vocal authority, Roosevelt imposed a strict ban on presidential impersonation on the air. . . .

As a result of the broadcast, Roosevelt also recognized the political value of securing Welles's services for radio campaign work during his third- and fourth-term bids. During the 1944 election, Welles traveled the eastern seaboard delivering endorsements at pro-FDR rallies, and he played a key role in the success of the election eve radio extravaganza, work for which he was gratefully commended by the president. In return, Roosevelt encouraged Welles's own political aspirations when the latter considered running for a senate seat in Wisconsin. . . .

Welles was also the object of considerable commercial attention after the broadcast. While the *Mercury Theater*'s sustaining status had been based upon its supposedly low audience appeal, the mammoth extent of the panic had demonstrated that the number of listeners who tuned in to the program, even on a casual basis, was far higher than originally assumed. The notoriety the program received after the "War of the Worlds" increased ratings even more (although never to the point of rivaling Charlie McCarthy). The week after the broadcast, the *Mercury Theater* attracted its first sponsor, Campbell Soup, and became the *Campbell Playhouse.*

Another significant lesson derived from the Welles broadcast was that the United States of 1938 was woefully unprepared for an actual war. The *Times* of London caustically remarked, "Here is a nation which, alone of big nations, has deemed it unnecessary to rehearse for protection against attack from the air by fellow beings on earth, and suddenly believes itself faced with a more fearful attack from another world." Government officials, army chiefs, and national defense heads expressed the view that, besides "revealing the jittery state of nerves brought on by war clouds over Europe," the broadcast "drove home how little prepared the nation was to cope with an abrupt emergency." According to the *New York Times*, on the "mere suggestion of a foreign attack" the United States erupted into a panic, causing "thousands from one end of the country to the other to be frightened out of their senses, starting an incipient flight of hysterical refugees, taxing the police and hospitals, confusing traffic and choking the usual means of communication." What would the American people have done if this had been a genuine invasion? What would happen if the Luftwaffe developed a heavy bomber capable of reaching New York or Washington? H.G. Wells [the British novelist and author of *The War of the Worlds*] was astonished that Americans reacted as they did, despite not having "the war right under [their] chimneys" as Britain had. Dorothy Thompson wrote:

> Even though Hitler had managed to scare Europe to its knees during the Munich Crisis, he at least had a powerful army and air force to back up his threatening words. By contrast, Mr. Welles scared thousands into demoralization with nothing at all.

Welles's broadcast drew public attention to the dangers of international detachment. In fact, . . . many Americans now renounced isolationism and rallied behind the president's defense campaign. . . .

As the U.S. began to assume a more active role in the European conflict, shortwave broadcasts from belligerent sources were heavily curtailed by the Roosevelt Administration. As *Broadcasting* noted:

> While all warring governments would be glad to furnish speakers to address American radio audiences, the strict censorship and abundance of propaganda makes the acceptance of such broadcasts a risky business, which might result in an emotional reaction similar to that caused by the Martian drama.

. . . Despite these precautions, the dictators continued to direct a steady stream of pro-Axis propaganda into United States airspace. The day after the Welles program, Mussolini commenced the operation of a new imperial radio center near Rome. With eight of the world's most powerful transmitters (of 100 kilowatts each) using 22 separate wavelengths, the center was specifically designed to beam "fascist thought to the Americas," and to "echo faithfully the pulsing life of the new Italy" across the globe.

The Credibility Gap

Another result of the broadcast was a noticeable, if temporary, decrease of credulity among the American public with regard to what they heard on the radio. Howard Koch remarked that "if the non-existent Martians . . . had anything to teach us, I believe it is the virtue of doubting and testing everything that comes to us over the airwaves and on the printed page."

Because of this new tendency to suspend belief, many observers feared that "should a real catastrophe take place, people may take it as another hoax, in spite of urgent pleas by the authorities to the contrary." Their fears were justified. A little more than three years after America was invaded by Martians, it was attacked—this time in reality—by another foreign foe, and the public reacted to the radio announcement with skepticism. Ironically, the morning of the attack on Pearl Harbor, Welles was on the air reading from the works of Walt Whitman, when his program was interrupted with a news flash. Listeners were inclined to dismiss the news as another Welles trick. One listener remembered:

> The radio was on. It was a quiet, tranquil Sunday afternoon. And then the announcer broke in: "The Japanese have attacked Pearl Harbor." My first question was, "Is this another Orson Welles 'War of the Worlds' broadcast?"

When NBC's rooftop correspondent broadcast an eyewitness account of the raid to American listeners, he felt obliged to add an earnest assurance: "It's a real war, it's no joke!" According to *Broadcasting:*

> Nowhere did the straight radio reports of the terrific bombing of Honolulu—of Japanese pilots diving over the beautiful mountains to fire U.S. ships and kill U.S. men—create anything resembling the panic created three years ago by Orson Welles' famed faking of a Martian invasion.

Because of Welles's clever manipulation, Americans had "become so inured to tragedy" that even real war and likely invasion could not frighten them.

The Legacy Continues

Despite the renewed public awareness that resulted from the numerous inquiries, surveys, studies, and writings after the *War of the Worlds* broadcast, it was not beyond the realm of possibility that America could panic again. Indeed, the continued influence of radio, and then television, on the public consciousness made a repeat of October 30, 1938, even more likely.

In 1939, a similar type of script was enacted over a local station in Charleston, S.C. Entitled "Palmetto's Fantasy," the program dealt with a deadly anti-aircraft ray that went haywire and dropped into a nearby reservoir, killing hundreds of people and polluting the city's water supply. Even before the broadcast terminated, station WCSC, police, and newspapers in Charleston were deluged with calls from terrified listeners.

In 1940, a radio plug for a planetarium show, "How the World Will End," had scientists predicting that the life on earth would cease at 3:00 P.M. on April 1. Since it followed directly after a news program, this advertisement created a local panic in the small city where it originated, jamming switchboards and overburdening the police.

On a larger and more violent scale was the panic that resulted in Quito, Ecuador, in 1949, when the Welles program was translated into Spanish and a few local details were added. Listeners heard that the invaders were advancing upon the town from the south, destroying all opposition. An appeal by the "Minister of the Interior" for an organized defense on the program prompted one provincial governor to place his troops and police on full alert. The town's church bells were tolled, and local priests went into the streets seeking divine intervention. The South American program not only evoked the same hysterical response as its earlier American counterpart, but upon realizing they had been deceived, listeners burned down the radio station and killed or injured over twenty people, many of whom had acted in the drama. Rioting around the studio was so intense, order could be restored only through the intervention of tanks and tear-gas.

In a 1964 revision of his *Invasion from Mars: A Study in the Psychology of Panic*, Hadley Cantril stated his belief that late twentieth century society was not too sophisticated to be taken in again. Indeed, he maintained that a similar hoax could cause panic on an even more extensive scale. Even today, it seems possible. Since 1938, the world has witnessed the development of weapons of mass destruction "against which there appears little protection." With the 1969 moon landing and the development of universe-ranging satellites and radio telescopes, the earth no longer seems remote and inaccessible in space. Nightly newscasts frequently present the latest close-up photos of previously unviewed planetary bodies taken by the Hubble telescope. A Northwestern University psychologist has remarked: "I think we still have a mindset to be afraid of some unknown enemy and we've been socialized by a whole variety of movies and television shows to be open to the notion of extraterrestrial life—probably more than ever before." These factors could only "enhance the possibility of delusions that would be even more plausible than the invasion of Martians, and would not take the combined talents of H.G. Wells and Orson Welles to set it off."

Cantril's thesis seemed to have been proven in 1965, when a power failure caused a blackout in a New England city, and millions of "blind" citizens succumbed to feelings of fear that a missile had fallen and total destruction was imminent. In 1977, WPRO, Providence, presented a localized version of *War of the Worlds* that sparked a storm of protest from area listeners. During the great old-time radio revival of the seventies, as the Welles program became a Halloween staple for AM stations across the country, mini-panics of this sort occurred in countless localities (Buffalo, N.Y., being perhaps the most prominent). In 1982, a German television dramatization depicting an alien visitation propelled thousands of anxious people to their telephones to get emergency instructions. A few years later, a British news announcer interrupted a radio music program to announce that Russian missiles were over the Channel. Before he had an opportunity to explain that the bulletin was a promo for another program, listeners swamped the police with calls.

Despite these repeat performances, Cantril in 1964 felt that the Welles broadcast was unique in its effect on the American public. Television "could not compete with the scenes painted by the imaginations of frightened listeners, nor could it adequately picture all of the situations described in the broadcast." This could only be accomplished through radio. When CBS presented *Without Warning*, a modern television version of *War of the Worlds*, on October 30, 1994 (using the same bulletin-like format), the level of popular fright in no way approached that elicited on Halloween Eve 1938, despite the realistic additions of "live" video feeds, NASA computer simulations, satellite relays, and the employment of a very convincing Charles Kuralt–type anchor. But the fact that, in numerous localities across the United States, police stations and broadcast studios received calls from fearful viewers serves as potent testimony of the enduring power of Welles's manipulative formula. The public reaction in 1994 is all the more striking in view of the fact that viewers were given even more warning than their counterparts had received fifty years earlier. The modern recreation was not only listed in the newspaper and *T.V. Guide* weeks in advance, it was prefaced by a twenty-minute documentary discussing the Victorian novel and describing exactly how Welles had perpetrated his hoax. (For those who, against all odds, managed to miss every warning, CBS provided seven written and spoken disclaimers during the telecast itself.) Certainly popular credulity played a key role in eliciting a hysterical response in 1938, but the 1994 CBS production seems to reinforce the timeworn adage that as a society grows older, it does not necessarily grow wiser.

EVENT 13 The Rescue at Dunkirk Proves Hitler Can Be Resisted: May 1940

The Rescue at Dunkirk

by the *Times* (London)

Approximately 200,000 British and 140,000 French troops, including some Belgium troops, were evacuated over a five-day period off the northern coast of France at the port of Dunkirk while rapidly advancing German troops pursued them. The June 1940 drama took place under the constant threat of German Luftwaffe overhead and artillery aground. But with the aid of troops who stayed behind to set up lines of defense, so they could escape, and with the aid of military and local volunteers who ferried the men across the channel to British soil, the rescue was a remarkable success.

Boats of all kinds, from private motor boats and navy patrols to passenger ferries and large naval destroyers, were used to transport the stranded troops across the forty-mile-wide English Channel. Although thirty thousand troops either died in battle or were captured in the end, the British navy and army were still intact enough and of sufficient strength to regroup, as they would prove in their later defense in the Battle of Britain that July. As news of the latest developments at Dunkirk surfaced in May and June 1940, the news correspondents in the field for England's daily newspaper, the *Times*, kept England and others well informed. No one perhaps was more aware of the pending danger than England, for Nazi invasion appeared imminent. In the following article published in the *Times* in June 1940, the news correspondent retells the drama of the difficult escape that unfolded amidst dangerous battle. Stories of troops who marched more than forty miles in twenty-four hours to reach Dunkirk, of boat crews under constant attack, and of heroic local volunteers who provided boats, are among the stories told.

"Brigade That Did Not Yield," *The Times* (London), June 3, 1940, p. 3.

Tens of thousands of British and French soldiers continued to pour into England yesterday, and day and night the Navy is carrying on its brilliant work of rescue from Dunkirk in warships, transports, and craft of all kinds.

At 5 A.M. yesterday [June 2, 1940] a British infantry brigade was embarked from the beach north of Dunkirk. It had been in the midst of the fighting in Flanders from start to finish. It was among the troops which led the advance into Belgium; it fought in the rear-guard from the farthest front reached by the B.E.F. [British Expeditionary Force] to the gates of Dunkirk.

"My men," said the brigadier on stepping ashore in England, "never once gave way. They beat back every German attack, and every time they retreated it was when ordered and only as far as ordered." On one day the brigade marched over 40 miles in 24 hours.

Among those safely landed are increasing numbers of General Prioux's gallant French Army who had hacked their way through to Dunkirk. They were remarkably fit and confident. One of the small boats on its way across with a load of soldiers found time to stop and pick up two German airmen who had been shot down. They were landed as prisoners of war, and were given sandwiches and coffee before they were removed under escort.

Marched from the Quay

While many of the troops were ready to fall asleep the moment they entered the trains, several companies of a French regiment at one port marched off the landing quay with military precision, their colonel at their head. Hungry though they were, many of the French officers and men refused at first to accept the sandwiches offered them until they had been assured there was no food scarcity in England.

One of the volunteers who helped to ferry the troops home was a boy of 15, who took his regular place in his father's motor-boat. For three days and nights father and son made continuous trips across the Channel without rest.

Boys of 17 also left their work in South-East Coast towns to volunteer to man small vessels crossing to Dunkirk.

One said: "I was very frightened at first, but the soldiers were not frightened, and that bucked me up. Besides there were so many air attacks that after the first dozen or so we got used to them."

The crew of nine of a motor-boat, which under constant fire

ferried men from the beach at Dunkirk to the transports for three days and nights, included one man, aged 69—Charles Knight. The boat had towed across the Channel eight wherries containing cans of fresh water. Owing to the shallowness of the water it was arranged for eight soldiers at a time to wade out to the wherries and each wherry in turn delivered its load to the motor-boat, whence they were conveyed to larger ships. Many hundreds of men were successfully transported in this way throughout the night. As the last load was being carried the officer in command on the beach called out, "I can't see who you are; who are you?" On being told that they were members of the crew of a motor-boat from a South-East port the officer shouted back, "Thank God for such men as you." The motor-boat was riddled with shrapnel when it returned to England three days later.

Destroyer's Escape

One British destroyer, making her seventh crossing from Dunkirk, was attacked three times in an hour by waves of bombers.

"They were dropping bombs all around us," said one soldier, "but they never once hit the ship itself."

The soldiers on deck, though fully exposed to the attack, bore it unflinchingly. Bomb after bomb hit the water within a few yards of the ship, and as it burst threw tearing pieces of shrapnel across the decks, through the ranks of the men who were lying down in an effort to get what shelter they could. But though she had a number of dead and wounded, the destroyer reached England after having brought down at least two enemy bombers.

Tales of magnificent heroism were told by hundreds of Scottish soldiers who returned home to Glasgow and the West of Scotland during the week-end. It is characteristic of the spirit of these men that after describing the hell they had been through one of them added, "The joke was that we got the worst strafing of all in what was called a rest camp."

One young soldier said, "I'll never forget that beach at Dunkirk. Boats of every conceivable size and shape from rowing boats upwards were taking men off as fast as they could. The oil tanks in Dunkirk were blazing and German aeroplanes were roaring overhead unloading their bombs. Men were wading up to their necks to join the boats."

After he was taken on board the destroyer *Grafton*, the ship was sunk, he said, but the men in the destroyer were magnificent.

Soldiers and sailors alike sat about the deck calmly waiting, and there was no suggestion of panic.

Camerons' Stand

Stories of individual acts of bravery were told yesterday by men who have reached a London hospital. Company Quarter-Master Sergeant Higgs, of Leicester, who was blown up by a bomb and for a time paralysed, said that his battalion was withdrawing and had to pass through a large town where there was a battalion of Cameron Highlanders.

"We saw the Jocks in doorways and at corners with their bayonets," he said. " Whenever Jerry [a German] approached they just went for them. It was real hand-to-hand fighting. Several battalions withdrew safely through the town, and still the Camerons stuck it. It was a grand stand, and there is no doubt that it helped those other battalions to get away."

EVENT 13 **The Rescue at Dunkirk Proves Hitler Can Be Resisted: May 1940**

Dunkirk's Effect on World Opinion

by Patrick Wilson

Following the successful rescue of nearly 330,000 British soldiers at Dunkirk in May and June 1940, British prime minister Winston Churchill was quoted as saying, "We must be very careful not to assign to this the attributes of a victory. Wars are not won by evacuations." In the following article, author Patrick Wilson agrees with Churchill's words of caution.

Wilson begins with the tragic side of Dunkirk, the numbers of men actually wounded and killed in the defense of France. At the same time, he is quick to point out that although Germany achieved a great victory, it was hardly a defeat for Britain.

Patrick Wilson teaches history at Bradfield College in southern England. His recent book on prisoners of war, *War Behind the Wire*, was published in 2000. He has also written *Dunkirk: From Disaster to Deliverance* and has edited the diaries of an Australian teenager who fought in World War I.

'So long as the English tongue survives, the word Dunkirk will be spoken with reverence. In that harbour, such a hell on earth as never blazed before, at the end of a lost battle, the rags and blemishes that had hidden the soul of democracy fell away. There, beaten but unconquered, in shining splendour, she faced the enemy, this shining thing in the souls of free men, which [Adolf] Hitler cannot command. It is in the great tradition of democracy. It is a future. It is victory.'

New York Times, 1 June 1940

'For us Germans the word "Dunkirchen" will stand for all time for victory in the greatest battle of annihilation in history. But, for the British and French who were there, it will remind them for the rest of their lives of a defeat that was heavier than any army had ever suffered before.'

Der Adler, 5 June 1940

The Losses

Few of the men in the German Sixth Army, as they marched tentatively into the smoking ruins of Dunkirk on 4 June 1940, could have envisaged that the war would last another five years and that they would end up on the losing side. The British had capitulated and not even their subsequent remarkable evacuation could hide the scale of their defeat. Dishevelled, weary and weaponless, the men of the BEF [British Expeditionary Force] arrived back in England. Britain's material losses during the campaign had been astounding, with its army's stores and equipment strewn around Northern France. The Navy too had paid a heavy price for its heroics. Six destroyers, five minesweepers, eight transport ships and a further 200 vessels had been sunk, with an equal number badly damaged.

British casualties amounted to 68,000, while French losses totalled around 290,000 with many more than that either missing or taken prisoner. German casualties, on the other hand, amounted to 27,074 killed and 111,034 wounded. The statistics tell the story. Hitler had reason to be pleased with his forces, whose tactics, skill and fighting prowess had led to such a rout. His Order of the Day on 5 June stated:

> 'Soldiers of the West Front! Dunkirk has fallen . . . with it has created the greatest battle in world history. Soldiers! My confidence in you knows no bounds. You have not disappointed me.'

On the other side of the Channel [Prime Minister Winston] Churchill, too, was praising the efforts of his forces whilst warning that 'We must be very careful not to assign to this the attributes of a victory. Wars are not won by evacuations'.

Nevertheless the tact remained that, though Germany had achieved a total victory, Britain had not suffered a complete defeat. Churchill had predicted that 30,000 men could be lifted off, whilst Admiral Ramsay had hoped for 45,000. To everyone's astonishment the vast bulk of the army (around 330,000 men) had been rescued, and while Britain still had an army there was hope. The miracle of this deliverance lies in the number of extraordinary factors that made it possible. The decision of Gort (the commander of the BEF) to ignore Churchill and the French commanders and head to the coast, the halt order, the weather, the survival of the Eastern Mole (the pier from which the majority of troops were evacuated), and the incredible determination of the Royal Navy, all combined to save the BEF. General Guderian [of German command] later reflected, 'What the future of the war would have been like if we had succeeded in taking the British Expeditionary Force prisoners at Dunkirk is now impossible to guess.'

If Britain Had Surrendered

It seems almost certain that, if the evacuation from Dunkirk had not taken place, Churchill, with a quarter of a million men in captivity, would have been left with little option but to bow to pressure for peace terms to be signed. Without a large amount of its professional army, it is hard to see how Britain could have recovered. In fact, Hitler never wished to enter into a war with Britain. He admired the country whose Empire he believed powerfully reinforced his ideas of racial domination, commenting that 'To maintain their power at their side, only Germany can be that power.' After Dunkirk, however, he was stunned to find that his 'sensible peace arrangements' were continuously and categorically rejected. Even as late as 6 July Hitler insisted that the invasion of Britain would only be tried as a last resort 'if it cannot be made to sue for peace any other way'.

If the evacuation attempt had failed and Hitler's lenient peace treaty had been accepted, the outcome of the war would of course have been vastly different. Germany would have had extra resources—including the 40 divisions which Britain's continued hostility required in Africa and on the Atlantic Wall, as well as the 1,882 aircraft, and their experienced pilots and bomber crews, which were lost over Britain in the coming months. Faced by a Germany buoyed with these additional forces, Russia almost certainly would have fallen. Indeed, even without them the Germans managed to reach the outer defences of an evacuated Moscow by the first winter of the campaign, and that was after the fateful decision to delay the start of Operation Barbarossa until June 1941.

American Support Won

As significantly, Dunkirk aroused American sentiment. Epic accounts of the evacuation captured the public imagination and generated the first overt signs of popular and governmental support for Britain. The *Washington Evening Star*, the day after [Operation] Dynamo's conclusion, argued that 'It is a matter of inestimable importance to our own security that we should instantly remove all restrictions on the rendering of realistic, material aid to the Allies'. If Dunkirk had failed, if Britain had signed peace terms or if it had shown any signs of having its spirit broken, then the USA would have been much less prepared to enter what was essentially a European war. As it was, the effects of Dunkirk were instantaneous, and by mid-June some half a million rifles were on their way across the Atlantic. The whole episode, and Britain's reaction following it, had proved the resolve of the nation, which Churchill's speech further highlighted when he promised that Britain would preserve 'the whole world, including the United States' from sinking 'into the abyss of a new Dark Age'.

This was vital. As US Secretary of State Cordell Hull later commented, 'Had we any doubt of Britain's determination to keep on fighting we would not have taken steps to get material aid to her.' If this is the case then one can be absolutely certain that the USA would not have later provided Communist Russia with vital supplies. Yet if Dunkirk was to help gain Britain one ally, it lost her another. At 8:50 A.M. on 22 June France signed an armistice in the same wagon-lit at Rethondes, near Compiegne, where in November 1918 Marshal [Ferdinand] Foch had received the defeated German emissaries. Karl Heinz Mende summed up German feeling when he wrote home, 'The great battle in France is now ended. It lasted twenty-six years'. The revenge was complete and, following [French] General [Charles] Huntziger's signature, the site was razed.

Embittered France

A stunned French public could do little but bear witness to the speed of their country's collapse. Yet France searched for a scapegoat. Dunkirk had left the French feeling abandoned and embittered towards their Entente partner and crude propaganda pouring out from [Nazi propaganda minister Joseph] Goebbels' bureau in Berlin further fuelled the flames of resentment. Stories of

British troops forcing French soldiers out of boats and off the Mole abounded. The fact that over 102,000 of the 123,000 French troops rescued were lifted off by British vessels was ignored.

Desperate attempts prior to the Armistice on 22 June were made to keep the Alliance together. Indeed on 16 June [French general Charles] De Gaulle and Churchill had signed a 'Declaration of Union'. It did little, however, to disguise the mistrust and disillusionment that both nations now felt for each other. Britain had learnt the lesson that it should never again rely on other people's forces, and its post-war policy of building up an 'independent deterrent' of atomic weaponry reflected this. France, on the other hand, felt that Britain could not be relied upon militarily or economically if the going got tough. It was no coincidence that it was France, under De Gaulle, which vetoed Britain's applications to join the Common Market in the 1960s.

Britain Alone

In June 1940 Britain stood alone. For some, this was rather a relief. King George VI reflected such a sentiment in a letter to his mother, Queen Mary, on 27 June when he wrote, 'Personally I feel happier we have no allies to be polite to and to pamper'. A number of Generals, after their experiences in France, felt the same way. Churchillian grandiloquence played upon this 'Britain alone' theme: 'What has happened in France makes no difference to our actions and purpose. We have become the sole champions in arms to defend the world cause.' His rallying cries made an instant impression. Dunkirk had proved, with its much publicised civilian participation, that the war was more than a conflict between armies on the continent, the outcome of which the public were powerless to determine. The threat of invasion, along with the necessary myth of an army saved by the 'little boats', brought a nation together. A sense of involvement that had been lacking since the declaration of war now burst forth. Britain had sleep-walked into the war and it took the reverses in France and the evacuation to wake her from the complacency and overconfidence that existed prior to those events. Essentially, Dunkirk provided Britain with a second chance that had to be seized.

Churchill's Reputation Is Changed

Churchill's leadership of the country had been doubted prior to the evacuation. Many, including [former prime minister Neville]

Chamberlain, had favoured the less contentious [British foreign secretary] Halifax. General Ironside believed that Churchill did not have 'the stability for guiding others'. John Colville, a junior member of the prime ministerial staff, observed that:

> 'The mere thought of Churchill as Prime Minister sends a cold chill down the spines of the staff at 10 Downing Street. . . . His verbosity and restlessness made unnecessary work, prevented real planning and caused friction. Our feelings were widely shared in the Cabinet Office, the Treasury and throughout Whitehall.' [Churchill became Britain's prime minister May 10, 1940, prior to the Dunkirk evacuation.]

After Dunkirk his leadership was never questioned. The eloquence of his patriotic and determined rhetoric captured the mood of the nation and inspired the citizens of Britain to unwavering defiance of the Nazi peril.

Preparations for the defence of the island were instantaneous. By mid-July over a million men had enrolled in the Local Defence Volunteers (LDV). Roadblocks and pillboxes sprang up everywhere, signposts were rearranged or removed, barbed wire and beach fortifications were laid. This was total war. The country braced itself for imminent invasion. . . .

The Invasion of Britain

By 16 July Hitler had lost patience. In Directive No 126 he stated, 'As England, in spite of the hopelessness of her position, has so far shown herself unwilling to come to any compromise, I have decided to begin to prepare for, and if necessary carry out, an invasion of Britain'. But Hitler had, to borrow Chamberlain's earlier phrase, 'missed the bus'. It seems highly unlikely that Britain could have resisted a German invasion in early June. Churchill knew this and after his 'We shall fight them on the beaches' speech, reportedly covered up the BBC microphone and said, 'but we've only got bottles to do so'. Certainly the BEF was in no position to fight. On their return, brigades existed as names only and the nation, dazed by recent events, had virtually no preparations in place. The recently created LDV units, with pitch forks and the odd shotgun, would have provided little more than a spirited but futile resistance. The depleted Navy, as well as the RAF, was Britain's only hope, but the numerical supremacy of the Nazi forces provided Germany with a massive advantage.

Hitler's decision to delay gave the country much-needed time to prepare. He refused to listen to his Generals. . . .

An often-neglected consequence of the fighting leading up to Dunkirk was the effect it had on Hitler himself. His undeniably successful tactic of attacking through the Ardennes and his firm support of blitzkrieg tactics instilled a belief in him that as a military commander he was infallible. Hitler, the First World War Corporal, had proved that the caution of his Wehrmacht Generals was unfounded. Increasingly after Dunkirk, he made decisions that would have been best left to his commanders, and this was to have catastrophic effects during the Russian campaign.

The successful evacuation from Dunkirk was brushed aside. Had not the mighty France fallen? Hitler had defeated the great warrior nation with ease and, with the same ill founded optimism of Napoleon before him, he could see no reason why a similar lightning campaign in Russia would not have equal success. Such was his confidence that as Britain awoke to the reality and necessity of 'total' war following Dunkirk, Hitler actually began demobilising part of his own force and reduced his war productions.

The Myth of Dunkirk

All too often people just think of Dunkirk as the time when scores of patriotic citizens leapt into their small craft to aid their army in its hour of need. Certainly this occurred, but the truth is that most of the small craft were in the hands of a wide assortment of Naval personnel. Rarely do people think about the defence of the soldiers on the perimeter and strongpoints; nor do they give enough credit to the Royal Navy and the larger vessels that were responsible for rescuing the massive majority of troops. Dunkirk became a necessary myth, but its importance in shaping the course of World War Two has been vastly underestimated. Dunkirk was the beginning of the end for the Third Reich.

CHRONOLOGY

1920

January 10: The League of Nations is formed, a result of President Woodrow Wilson's Fourteen Points peace proposal at the end of World War I.
January 16: National Prohibition goes into effect prohibiting the manufacture or sale of alcoholic beverages. Sales of coffee, soft drinks, and ice cream sodas boom, but alcohol consumption and sales continue illegally.
March 19: The U.S. Senate rejects the Treaty of Versailles and membership in the League of Nations (the League Covenant was part of the treaty).
August 18: Tennessee ratifies the Nineteenth Amendment, satisfying the two-thirds vote majority needed by states for woman suffrage to become U.S. federal law. Proclaimed in effect August 26, 1920.
November 2: KDKA in Pittsburgh, Pennsylvania, becomes the world's first radio station to go on the air. Warren Harding's presidential election is broadcast.
November 15: The General Assembly of the League of Nations meets for the first time in Geneva, Switzerland.

1921

March 17: The Mothers' Clinic for Constructive Birth Control opens in London. The American Birth Control League is started by Margaret Sanger in the United States.
May 19: Congress passes the Dillingham Bill (Emergency Quota Act) to restrict immigration.
July 26–29: Adolf Hitler becomes leader of the German National Socialist Workers' Party.
September 8: Margaret Gorman is crowned the first Miss America in Atlantic City, New Jersey.
September 10: The Avus Autobahn, the world's first highway designed exclusively for motor vehicles and controlled access, officially opens in Berlin.

1922

February 6: A naval armaments treaty that restricts the size and weight of future ships built by the United States, Britain, France, Italy, and Japan for a ten-year period is established at the Washington Conference. Submarine warfare and the use of poison gas are also restricted.
February 15: The Permanent Court of International Justice opens at The Hague (seat of the Dutch government).
March 15: The Kingdom of Egypt is proclaimed. Britain terminates its protectorate over Egypt and Sultan Ahmed Fuad assumes new title as king.
October 28: Fascist dictatorship of Benito Mussolini begins in Italy after a successful takeover of the government ("March on Rome").
November 26: Egypt's tomb of King Tutankhamen discovered at Luxor in the Valley of the Kings by two Englishmen.

1923

January 2: The German mark drops to 7,260 to the U.S. dollar. Food prices rise and unemployment escalates to 1.5 million, causing considerable social unrest. By the end of November the mark is at an amazing 4.2 trillion to the dollar. Middle-class Germans lose their savings and pensions, while formerly affluent Germans must sell their possessions in exchange for food.
January 11: France and Belgium occupy the Ruhr after Germany fails to pay the reparations demanded of them in the Treaty of Versailles (1919).
April 19: The first baseball game is held in New York's Yankee Stadium. More than sixty thousand fans watch Babe Ruth hit a three-run homer in the third inning. The Yankees go on to win their first World Series, beating the New York Giants four games to two.
May 26: Jordan (Transjordania) is established as an autonomous state. The British protectorate occupies 80 percent of Palestinian territory and is headed by Emir Abdullah ibn Husein.
July 6: The Union of Soviet Socialist Republics (USSR) becomes a reality (areas included are Russia, the Ukraine, White Russia, and Transcaucasia).
July 10: Mussolini dissolves all non-Fascist parties in Italy, fur-

ther solidifying his dictatorship. A law is forced through parliament on November 14.
August 2: U.S. president Warren Harding dies of a massive stroke in San Francisco.
September 1: Tokyo and Yokohama are largely destroyed by Japan's great Kanto earthquake and fire. Some 100,000 are killed and 752,000 injured; 83,000 houses are destroyed and 380,000 damaged. A relief effort by the United States follows.
November 8: In Munich, Adolf Hitler fails in an attempted takeover of government, known as the Beer Hall Putsch. He is sent to prison where he writes his autobiography, *Mein Kampf.*

1924

January 21: Vladimir Lenin, premier of USSR (1917–1924) and Russian leader of the Communist revolution (1917), dies. Petrograd is renamed Leningrad in his honor. A power struggle between Josef Stalin and Leon Trotsky begins.
February 12: George Gershwin performs *Rhapsody in Blue* for the first time at New York's Aeolian Hall, accompanied by Paul Whiteman's orchestra.
May 26: Congress passes the Johnson-Reed Immigration Act, further restricting the quota of immigrants allowed from a particular country to 2 percent of that nationality living in the United States in 1890. The act is extremely offensive to the Japanese who are excluded from any immigration. Their ambassador warns of "grave consequences."
June 10: Mussolini's Fascisti murder Italian Socialist deputy Giacomo Matteotti, who had described the Fascisti's illegal acts of violence in his book *The Fascisti Exposed.*
August 18: French troops begin to withdraw from the Ruhr.
September 1: The Dawes Plan goes into effect, which sets the amount of reparations owed by Germany. It also provides an Allied loan of 800 million gold marks (110 million to come from the United States).
October 5: "Little Orphan Annie" by cartoonist Harold Lincoln Gray debuts in the *New York Daily News*. Its message is political and speaks out against communism, liberalism, and other threats to free enterprise and rugged individualism.

1925

March 12: China's republican leader Sun Yat-sen dies, followed by political unrest and demonstrations. At year's end, General Chiang Kai-shek is commander in chief of Sun's army and manages to defeat Sun's opponent Chen Chiung-ming and bring the region under control.

March 13: In the Scopes Monkey Trial in Dayton, Tennessee, schoolteacher John Scopes, defended by Clarence Darrow, is prosecuted by William Jennings Bryan for teaching evolution in a public school. He is found guilty and fined one hundred dollars.

March 18: The worst tornado in U.S. history kills 689 and injures thousands, cutting through the states of Missouri, Illinois, and Indiana and resulting in millions of dollars in damage.

March 22: Tokyo Shibaura, Japan's first radio station, goes on the air.

April 25: Paul von Hindenburg becomes president of Germany.

August 8: The Ku Klux Klan parade in Washington, D.C., is the biggest demonstration in Klan history. Forty thousand Klan members garbed in white hoods and robes march down Pennsylvania Avenue in a show of strength, but their membership is declining.

November 28: The *Grand Ole Opry* makes its radio debut on WSM in Nashville, Tennessee.

December 12: The first motel, James Vail's Motel Inn, opens in San Luis Obispo, California. It accommodates 160 guests.

1926

Chiang Kai-shek becomes leader of China's revolutionary party. After taking Wuchang in October, he establishes the city as his seat of power.

January 8: Abdul-Aziz ibn Saud proclaims himself king of Hejaz and renames it Saudi Arabia.

March 16: Robert H. Goddard launches the first liquid-fueled rocket, ushering in the modern era of rocketry. His device will lead directly to the German V-2 rocket of World War II and the *Apollo* moon landing.

April 15: Charles Lindbergh initiates the first regularly scheduled mail flight between St. Louis and Chicago. He is the chief pilot for Robertson Aircraft.

May 9: U.S. Navy explorer Richard Evelyn Byrd and pilot Floyd Bennett leave Spitzbergen, Norway, in a trimotor Fokker monoplane and fly seven hundred miles to the North Pole, circle the pole thirteen times, and return in 15.5 hours.

July–October: Joseph Stalin becomes dictator of the Soviet Union and will rule for twenty-seven years. The Soviets will experience repression under his rule and their neighbors will encounter terror. Leon Trotsky and Grigori Zinoviev are expelled by the Politburo in October.
August 6: Harry Houdini, magician and escape artist, demonstrates his breath control by surviving underwater for ninety-one minutes in an airtight case with enough air to last five or six minutes. He later dies of an unrelated stomach injury on October 31. New Yorker Gertrude Ederle becomes the world's first woman to swim the English Channel. The Olympic champion crosses the channel in 14.5 hours and beats the world record by 2 hours. She suffers permanent hearing loss in the end.

1927

January 7: Transatlantic telephone service begins between New York and London at $75 or £15 for a three-minute conversation.
April 7: Television is first demonstrated by AT&T at New York's Bell Telephone Laboratories. Viewers see Commerce Secretary Herbert C. Hoover in his office at the capitol and hear him speak over telephone wires.
May 21: Charles Lindbergh flies his single-engine monoplane the *Spirit of St. Louis* from New York to Paris, completing the first solo transatlantic nonstop flight.
August 23: Despite worldwide efforts to have charges dropped for lack of evidence, Nicola Sacco and Bartolomeo Vanzetti are executed for their alleged role in a payroll robbery and killing in 1920 at a South Braintree, Massachusetts, factory.
September 30: Baseball favorite Babe Ruth hits his sixtieth home run of the season, a record that will stand for thirty years.
October 6: Warner Brothers' full-length film *The Jazz Singer* with music and dialogue debuts and wows audiences in New York. Starring Al Jolson, *The Jazz Singer* is the first talking picture to achieve such success and marks the end of silent film.

1928

March 19: Radio comedy *Amos 'n' Andy* debuts on Chicago's WMAQ. The popular fifteen-minute show airs nationally the next year and attracts 40 million listeners.
May 12: Mussolini's Fascist government ends woman suffrage

in Italy. Only men age twenty-one and over are eligible to vote, reducing the electorate by around 7 million.
June 17–18: Amelia Earhart is the first woman to fly across the Atlantic as a passenger (two men pilot the plane). In 1932, she will make her own solo flight.
July 2: British women gain the right to vote.
August 27: Sixty-three nations sign the Kellogg-Briand Pact renouncing war. Designed by U.S. secretary of state Frank B. Kellogg and French foreign minister Aristide Briand, it is implemented by the League of Nations in September.
October 15: Germany's dirigible *Graf Zeppelin* travels 6,630 miles across the ocean to Lakehurst, New Jersey, in 121 hours on its first commercial flight, inaugurating transatlantic flight in lighter-than-air craft.
December 6: Bolivia and Paraguay go to war over the Chaco territory. Paraguay appeals to the League of Nations for help, but skirmishes continue until April 1929.

1929

January 9: Alexander Fleming performs the first clinical application of crude penicillin at St. Mary's Hospital in London. He treats a man suffering from a sinus infection and successfully destroys most of the staphylococci.
February 6: The Kellogg-Briand Pact is accepted by Germany.
February 11: Mussolini and the Pope Pius XI sign the Lateran Treaty, after a long church-state battle in Italy. An independent Vatican State is established.
February 14: Seven members of the "Bugs" Moran gang are wiped out in the "St. Valentine's Day massacre" in Chicago, as mobsters compete for control of the bootleg liquor trade. Al Capone's gang is suspected.
May 27: Charles Lindbergh and Anne Spencer Morrow are married.
July 17: Physicist and rocket scientist Robert H. Goddard launches the first rocket with a scientific payload (barometer and camera) at Auburn, Massachusetts. The publicity generated and a call to the state fire marshal results in the delay of future tests for several months.
August: In the first large-scale attack on Jews by Arabs over use of Jerusalem's Wailing Wall, many Jews are killed.

October 3: The Kingdom of the Serbs, Croats, and Slovenes becomes Yugoslavia.
October 29: Often referred to as "Black Tuesday," the U.S. stock market crashes. A record 16.4 million shares are traded and, despite assurances by trusted economists that a depression is not in the forecast, the slide continues and speculators who bought on margin are forced to sell, losing 30 billion dollars.
December 31: Guy Lombardo and his Royal Canadians play dance music at New York's Roosevelt Hotel on New Year's Eve, a tradition that will continue for decades.

1930

January 20: The radio drama, *The Lone Ranger*, debuts on Detroit's WXYZ. The opening song is the popular overture from Rossini's 1829 opera *Guillaume Tell.*
February 18: Astronomers in Flagstaff, Arizona, discover the planet Pluto.
March 12: Mahatma Gandhi's civil disobedience campaign against British control begins. He leads a 165-mile march to the Arabian Sea where he and his followers collect seawater and evaporate it into salt in direct defiance of the British salt laws.
May 19: South African white women gain the right to vote, but black men and women remain disenfranchised.
June 17: The United States signs the Smoot-Hawley Tariff Act, which will begin the European tariff war. Tariffs are at the highest levels in history.
October 5: The British dirigible R-101 burns northwest of Paris during its maiden voyage to Australia. Fifty-four lives are lost.
October 20: The Passfield Paper on Palestine is presented, suggesting a halt of Jewish immigration to Palestine due to unemployment among the Arabs.
December 11: New York's Bank of the United States, including sixty of its branches, closes, affecting four hundred thousand depositors. More than thirteen hundred banks will close in 1930.

1931

March 3: Congress makes "The Star Spangled Banner" the U.S. national anthem.
May 1: New York's Empire State Building opens. The 102-story skyscraper will be the world's tallest building for more than forty years.

July–August: German banks are hit with closures and bankruptcies.
September 19: Japan occupies Manchuria (northern China).
October 11: Hitler and Germany's Nationalist leader Hugenberg form an alliance.
October 24: Chicago mobster Al Capone is found guilty of income tax evasion and is sentenced to prison for eleven years.
December 7: Hunger marchers petition the White House for employment at a guaranteed minimum wage but are turned away. U.S. unemployment has reached 8 million.

1932

March 1: The twenty-month-old son of aviation pioneer Charles Lindbergh and his wife Anne is kidnapped. Lindbergh pays a ransom of fifty thousand dollars for Charles Lindbergh Jr.'s return but the child's body is found two months later. The world mourns the couple's loss.
March 7: Congress votes to give 40 million bushels of wheat held by the Federal Farm Bureau to needy Americans with distribution handled by the Red Cross.
April 19: Rocket scientist Robert H. Goddard launches a rocket with the first gyro-control apparatus used in rocket flight, developed by Goddard in New Mexico.
September 20: Mahatma Gandhi initiates a "fast unto death" to protest the British government's treatment of India's "untouchables." After six days of fasting a pact is made that improves the untouchables' status.

1933

January 30: Adolf Hitler becomes chancellor of Germany and will rule for twelve years. His rise to power comes on the tide of rising social and economic unrest and German nationalism.
February 15: An attempt is made on President-elect Franklin D. Roosevelt's life in Miami, Florida, by Giuseppe Zangara.
February 27: The German Reichstag is burned in Berlin. The Nazis use this as an excuse to restrict civil liberties.
March 4: President Franklin D. Roosevelt is inaugurated. With personal incomes 40 percent below 1929 levels, the nation's banks in collapse, and 15 million unemployed, the nation is inspired by Roosevelt's inaugural "call to action." This is the beginning of Roosevelt's New Deal.

March 5: President Roosevelt declares a nationwide bank holiday.
March 6: Congress passes the Emergency Banking Act, giving Roosevelt control over banking transactions and foreign exchange. Banks undergo examination and begin to reopen as permitted on March 13.
March 12: President Roosevelt's first "fireside chat" is broadcast on the radio.
March 20: Germany opens the first concentration camp at Dachau near Munich. It is designated for Jews, gypsies, and political prisoners.
March 23: Hitler is given full dictatorial power under the Enabling Act.
April 1: A national boycott of Jewish businesses begins in Nazi Germany.
May 12: The Federal Emergency Relief Act by Congress establishes a $500 million fund for distribution as grants to states.
July 14: The Nazi regime suppresses all political parties in Germany.
October 14: Germany announces it will withdraw from the League of Nations following Japan's announcement it will withdraw in 1935.
December 5: Utah becomes the thirty-sixth state to ratify the Twenty-first Amendment repealing the Eighteenth Amendment. Prohibition ends after an estimated 1.4 billion gallons of hard liquor have been sold illegally.

1934

March 31: The Civilian Conservation Corps (CCC) created by Congress will provide work for 3 million young men over the next eight years.
May 28: The world's first quintuplets (five girls) are born in Ontario, Canada, to Elzire Dionne.
June 10: The Federal Communications Commission (FCC) is created by Congress to supervise the U.S. telephone, telegraph, and radio industries.
June 30: Adolf Hitler eliminates German S.A. leaders and other rivals in a blood purge that kills at least seventy-seven party members.
July 25: Austrian premier Engelbert Dollfuss is murdered but the German Nazi coup is unsuccessful.

August 2: Paul von Hindenburg dies and Hitler becomes president (*der Führer*) of Germany.
September 18: The Soviet Union joins the League of Nations.
September 20: New York police arrest German American Bruno Richard Hauptmann for the murder of Charles Lindbergh Jr. Hauptmann is in possession of ransom money paid for the child's return but he denies any connection with the murder.

1935

March 16: Hitler rejects the disarmament clauses of the Versailles Treaty.
August 14: The Social Security Act is signed into law, which will provide old-age annuities and unemployment insurance benefits to Americans.
September 15: The Nuremberg Laws make persecution of German Jews legal, depriving them of German citizenship and intermarriage with "Aryans," who are regarded as the superior race.
October 3: Mussolini's Italian troops invade Ethiopia with Hitler's support.
November 18: Economic sanctions are imposed on Italy by the League of Nations for its invasion of Ethiopia.

1936

March 7: Germany occupies the Rhineland unopposed.
July 18: An army revolt against the republic led by generals Francisco Franco and Emilio Mola touches off a civil war in Spain. Both the Germans and Italians will provide military support.
October 25: Hitler and Mussolini form the Rome-Berlin Axis.
November 25: Japan signs the Anti-Comintern Pact with Germany. This agreement emphasizes their mutual hostility against communism and the Soviet Union, and provides a means of support should conflict arise. The pact is broken when Germany signs the Nazi-Soviet Pact in 1939.

1937

April 26: The German bombing of the Spanish Basque town Guernica inspires an angry Pablo Picasso to paint his protest mural *Guernica*.
May 6: Germany's new dirigible the *Hindenburg* explodes and

burns at Lakehurst, New Jersey, killing thirty-six passengers and ending the era of transatlantic travel by airship.
May 28: Neville Chamberlain becomes prime minister of Britain.
July 2: Aviator Amelia Earhart vanishes without a trace in her flight over the Pacific.
July 7: Japan invades China and captures Beijing, Shanghai, and Nanjing.
July 16: Germany opens Buchenwald concentration camp, which will hold 238,980 prisoners, mostly Jews; 56,545 will die in gas chambers.
December 11: Italy withdraws from the League of Nations.

1938

January 10: Still in China after their 1937 victories, the Japanese take Qingda (Tsingtao).
March 14: Germany annexes Austria. Britain and France continue their policy of appeasement by allowing Hitler to take Sudentenland without protest. That year the Nazis increase their persecution of Austrian Jews, plundering Jewish shops and homes.
May 26: The dedication of the first Volkswagen factory, commissioned by Adolf Hitler, takes place in Germany. Eventually, more than 18 million low-cost "beetles" will be sold.
July 11: Japanese and Russians clash at the Chinese-Siberian border.
September 23: Charles Lindbergh writes to the U.S. ambassador to Britain, "I am convinced that it is wiser to permit Germany eastward expansion than to throw England and France unprepared into a war at this time." Lindbergh has lived abroad since his son's 1932 murder. He has made surveys of British, German, and Soviet airpower.
October 30: The "War of the Worlds" airs on radio over CBS, convincing U.S. listeners that a Martian invasion has actually occurred, demonstrating the dramatic power of radio.
November 9: The worst massacre in German history follows the assassination of a German embassy official in Paris by a seventeen-year old German-born Polish Jew who has learned of the mistreatment of thousands of Polish Jews, including his family. The *Kristalnacht* riots follow, in which the Nazis loot, demolish, and burn Jewish buildings and homes, and carry off be-

tween twenty thousand and thirty thousand Jews to concentration camps.

December 18: The first nuclear fission of uranium is produced by German chemist Otto Hahn. News of the discovery spreads to other physicists who notice that the fission of uranium gives off extra neutrons, which can in turn split other uranium atoms, starting a chain reaction. In theory, the energy could be harnessed to make a powerful bomb.

1939

March 28: Spanish civil war ends with the fall of Madrid to Francisco Franco. Germany and Italy withdraw their forces.

April 9: Singer Marian Anderson is refused the use of a concert facility in Washington, D.C., because she is black. Eleanor Roosevelt and numerous others protest. The concert takes place at the Lincoln Memorial instead and is a resounding success.

May 13: The plight of the *St. Louis* begins. With 937 Jewish refugees aboard who have fled Nazi persecution, the ship is unable to find a welcome port. The U.S. Immigration Act of 1924 prevents entry. The ship heads back to Germany until Britain, France, Belgium, and Holland finally help, although most of the refugees will die within six years.

May 17: Jewish immigration to Palestine is limited to fifty thousand for the next five years by the British, who rule Palestine under a League of Nations mandate.

June 28: The first commercial transatlantic passenger air service leaves New York for France via Pan American Airway's *Dixie Clipper.* The flight takes 26.5 hours.

August 2: Albert Einstein sends a letter to President Roosevelt informing him of Germany's atomic research and their potential for creating a nuclear bomb.

August 23: Germany and Soviet Russia sign a nonaggression pact, allowing Germany to invade Poland on September 1.

September 3: England and France declare war on Germany and World War II begins.

September 17: Charles Lindbergh goes on U.S. radio to give his first anti-intervention speech concerning the war, arguing that Stalin is as much a threat as Hitler.

September 17: Soviets invade Poland from the east. Poland is partitioned between the USSR and Germany on September 28.

November 30: The Soviets invade Finland.

1940

April 9: Germany invades Norway and Denmark, and they surrender.
May 10: Winston Churchill succeeds Neville Chamberlain as Britain's prime minister after Chamberlain's resignation following criticism in the House of Commons. Germany begins its invasion of the Netherlands, Luxembourg, Belgium, and France. Belgium, the Netherlands, and Luxembourg fall in May, and France falls in June.
May 19–June 4: The heroic rescue operation known as "Operation Dynamo," of British and Allied troops begins at Dunkirk during the German invasion of France; 340,000 are rescued.
June 10: Italy declares war on France and Britain.
June 22: France signs an armistice with Germany, which divides France into an occupied and an unoccupied (Vichy) zone.
June 27: The Soviets invade Romania.
June 28: Congress passes the Alien Registration Act (Smith Act), which requires that aliens be fingerprinted. It also becomes unlawful to advocate the overthrow of the U.S. government or to belong to a group that similarly advocates an overthrow.
July 10: The Battle of Britain begins when the German Luftwaffe begins dropping thousands of bombs on British soil. In an all-out attack in September hundreds of Britons rush to air raid shelters underground when sirens blow but hundreds die nightly during attacks. In November, air raids will kill more than 4,550 Britons. The bombing lasts through March 1941 but the German invasion never materializes.
October 29: The first peacetime military draft in U.S. history begins.
November 5: Roosevelt is reelected president with 54 percent of the popular vote.
December 29: In a "fireside chat" President Roosevelt tells Americans that the United States "must be the great arsenal of democracy."

FOR FURTHER RESEARCH

General Reading

Frederick Lewis Allen, *The Big Change: America Transforms Itself: 1900–1950.* Westport, CT: Greenwood Publishing, 1983.

———, *Since Yesterday: The 1930s in America: September 3, 1929–September 3, 1939.* New York: Harper and Brothers, 1939.

Alistair Cooke, *Alistair Cooke's America.* New York: Alfred A. Knopf, 1973.

Arthur S. Link and William B. Catton, *American Epoch: A History of the United States Since 1900.* Vol. 2. New York: Alfred A. Knopf, 1973.

Carroll W. Pursell Jr., ed., *Technology in America: A History of Individuals and Ideas.* Cambridge, MA: MIT Press, 1981.

T.H. Watkins, *The Great Depression: America in the 1930s.* Boston: Little, Brown, 1993.

Harvey Wish, *Contemporary America: The National Scene Since 1900.* New York: Harper and Brothers, 1945.

Nineteenth Amendment and Woman Suffrage History

Margaret Chute, *The Green Tree of Democracy.* New York: Dutton, 1971.

Eleanor Flexner, *Century of Struggle: The Woman's Rights Movement in the United States.* New York: Atheneum, 1972.

Marjorie Spruill Wheeler, ed., *One Woman, One Vote: Rediscovering the Woman Suffrage Movement.* Troutdale, OR: NewSage Press and Educational Film Company, 1995.

Nancy Woloch, *Women and the American Experience: A Concise History.* New York: McGraw-Hill, 1996.

League of Nations and U.S. Foreign Policy

James Avery Joyce, *Broken Star: The Story of the League of Nations (1919–1920).* Amherst, NY: Prometheus Books, 1978.

Emily S. Rosenberg, "Twenties/Twenties Hindsight," *Foreign Policy*, September 2000.

Raymond J. Sontag, *A Broken World: 1919–1939.* New York: Harper & Row, 1971.

John C. Vinson, *Referendum for Isolation. Defeat of Article Ten of the League of Nations Covenant.* Athens: University of Georgia Press, 1961.

Fascism and Mussolini

Martin Blinkhorn, *Mussolini and Fascist Italy*. New York: Methuen, 1984.

Alexander De Grand, *Italian Fascism: Its Origins and Development.* Lincoln: University of Nebraska Press, 1982.

DISCovering World History, "Mussolini's 'March on Rome,' October 24, 1922–October 29, 1922," Gale Research, 1997. Reproduced in Student Resource Center. Farmington Hills, MI: Gale Group. December 2000. http://galenet.galegroup.com.

Simonetta Falasca-Zamponi, *Fascist Spectacle: The Aesthetics of Power in Mussolini's Italy.* Berkeley: University of California Press, 1997.

H.R. Kedward, *Fascism in Western Europe 1900–1945*. New York: New York University Press, 1971.

Charles Lindbergh

Charles A. Lindbergh, *Autobiography of Values.* New York: Harcourt Brace Jovanovich, 1978.

———, *The Spirit of St. Louis.* New York: Scribner, 1953.

Thomas Lowell and Thomas Lowell Jr., *Famous First Flights That Changed History.* Garden City, NY: Doubleday, 1969.

Leonard Mosley, *Lindbergh: A Biography.* New York: Doubleday, 1976.

The Jazz Singer and Sound in Film

Gene Brown, ed., *The New York Times Encyclopedia of Film: 1896–1928.* New York: Times Books, 1984.

Scott Eyman, *The Speed of Sound.* New York: Simon & Schuster, 1997.

Benjamin B. Hampton, *History of the American Film Industry: From Its Beginnings to 1931.* New York: Dover, 1970.

Robert H. Stanley, *The Celluloid Empire: A History of the American Motion Picture Industry.* New York: Hastings House, 1978.

U.S. Stock Market Crash

Frederick Lewis Allen, *Only Yesterday: An Informal History of the 1920s.* New York: Harper and Brothers, 1931.

Caroline Bird, *The Invisible Scar.* New York: D. McKay, 1966.

Economist, "A Refresher on the 1930s," September 19, 1998.

Robert Sobel, *Panic on Wall Street: A History of America's Financial Disasters.* New York: Macmillan, 1968.

Mahatma Gandhi

Yogesh Chadha, *Gandhi: A Life.* New York: John Wiley & Sons, 1997.

Louis Fischer, *The Life of Mahatma Gandhi.* New York: Harper & Row, 1950.

M.K. Gandhi, *Gandhi's Autobiography: The Story of My Experiments with Truth by M.K. Gandhi.* Washington, DC: Public Affairs Press, 1960.

Adolf Hitler

Alan Bullock, *Hitler, A Study in Tyranny.* New York: Harper & Row, 1962.

Ian Kershaw, *Hitler, 1889–1936: Hubris.* New York: W.W. Norton, 1999.

Robert Payne, *The Life and Death of Adolf Hitler.* New York: Praeger, 1973.

John Toland, *Adolf Hitler.* New York: Doubleday, 1976.

Franklin D. Roosevelt

James R. Chiles, "Bang! Went the Doors of Every Bank in America," *Smithsonian*, April 1997.

Kenneth S. Davis, *FDR: The New Deal Years, 1933–1937.* New York: Random House, 1986.

Frank Freidel, *Franklin D. Roosevelt: Launching the New Deal.* Boston: Little, Brown, 1973.

Robert S. McElvaine, *Origins of the Great Depression 1929–1941.* New York: Times Books, 1984.

Thomas Lunsford Stokes, *Chip off My Shoulder.* Princeton, NJ: Princeton University Press, 1940.

Prohibition

Edward Behr, *Prohibition: Thirteen Years That Changed America.* New York: Arcade, 1996.

Allan S. Everest, *Rum Across the Border: The Prohibition Era in Northern New York.* Syracuse, NY: Syracuse University Press, 1978.

Kenneth D. Rose. *American Women and the Repeal of Prohibition.* New York: New York University Press, 1996.

Pablo Picasso

Anthony Blunt, *Picasso's* Guernica. London: Oxford University Press, 1969.

Pierre Cabanne, *Pablo Picasso: His Life and Times.* Trans. Harold J. Salemson. New York: William Morrow, 1977.

Roland Penrose, *Picasso: His Life and Work.* Berkeley and Los Angeles: University of California Press, 1981.

"The War of the Worlds" and Radio's Influence

Frank Brady, *Citizen Welles: A Biography of Orson Welles.* New York: Scribner, 1989.

Robert J. Brown, *Manipulating the Ether: The Power of Broadcast Radio in Thirties America.* Jefferson, NC: McFarland, 1998.

John Houseman, *Run-Through.* New York: Simon & Schuster, 1972.

Howard Koch, *The Panic Broadcast: Portrait of an Event.* Boston: Little, Brown, 1970.

Dunkirk Battle and Rescue

The Battle of Britain, "Mass Evacuation from Dunkirk." www.battleofbritain.net.

John Carey, ed., *Eyewitness to History.* Cambridge, MA: Harvard University Press, 1988.

Winston Churchill, *Their Finest Hour.* Boston: Houghton Mifflin, 1949.

Richard Collier, *The Sands of Dunkirk.* New York: Dell, 1962.

Walter Lord, *Miracle of Dunkirk.* New York: Viking, 1982.

INDEX